NATHANIEL B. PALMER

Nineteenth Century Master Mariner

Harry F. Martin

Published by Historic Stonington
Stonington, Connecticut 2024

TABLE *of* CONTENTS

To my superbly supportive wife, Susan

ACKNOWLEDGEMENTS

Historic Stonington's (HS) Elizabeth Wood, Chelsea Mitchell, and Adi Ignatius
HS Executive Director Elizabeth Wood's strong early belief in me provided the support required to tell Nathaniel Palmer's story. Liz maintained her commitment throughout. Chelsea, director of HS's Woolworth Library, constantly made "unavailable material" available. She found needed sources and illustrations and helped craft the book's initial sections. Board President Adi Ignatius provided worldly guidance.

Mary M. Thacher and Rodney Johnstone
Mary Thacher's deep mastery of the importance of the relationships between Stonington's seafaring founding families, her detailed genealogical reports, her transcription of handwritten family papers in the Library of Congress and elsewhere, and her insistence I get the story right was a needed, dynamic stimulus.

Maritime advisor Rodney Johnstone kept Stonington on the world's sailing map by designing and building J Boats known to performance sailors everywhere. Rod helped me appreciate the great contribution Captain Palmer made to the development of America's role as a major maritime player in the nineteenth century.

Stuart Vyse
Stuart Vyse's background as an accomplished author and professional editor provided the constructive criticism needed to ensure this biography flowed smoothly for the reader. He insisted on proper sourcing for every key element and found our fine copy editor. His constant wise counsel made this a better book.

James Tertius De Kay
Stonington's naval historian wrote a definitive, thoughtful account of the origin and outcome of the British Royal Navy attack on Stonington in the War of 1812, *The Battle of Stonington, Torpedoes, Submarines, and Rockets in the War of 1812.*

Wil Bradford and Extended Families
Wil, representing descendants of the Bradford-Fanning families,

graciously provided permission to use quotes from their papers on loan to the HS Library, and extended family correspondence and his portraits of Edmund Fanning, Juliet Fanning, and Sarah Bradford.

Norman F. Boas, MD, RIP
Thanks to Dr. Boas's family for permission to use the former HS librarian, historian, and author's informative works: *Stonington during the American Revolution* and *Capt. N.B. Palmer & N.B. Palmer, 2nd—A Poignant Story*, Stonington, CT, 1998.

Michael Wiseman
The Commodore Emeritus of the Stonington Harbor Yacht Club (SHYC) described how Nathaniel Palmer sailed the forty-seven-foot sloop *Hero* ten thousand miles down the Atlantic to the Falkland Islands without the ability to sight longitude simply by using Plane Sailing.

Mark Scott
Blue-water sailor on the SHYC Board, Mark wrote our *Ships Glossary* explaining qualities of the various vessels Nathaniel Palmer captained. His knowledge of the world's winds, currents, and ship's architecture was invaluable.

Susan Lindberg
Graphic designer who designed, laid out, and prepared the book for publication.

ABC Photo Lab, Mystic CT
Liz and Dana helped create the inspired first draft printing of this book.

Julia Lavarnway
My wonderful copy-line editor in far-away Buffalo, NY, always skillful, patient, and helpful.

Sue Fornara
Graphic designer who assisted in the creation of the *Ships Glossary* and *Maps*.

Kendra Mills
Our authoritative index editor.

FOREWORD

Harry Martin gives new relevance and meaning to the life of Captain Nathaniel Brown Palmer, Nineteenth Century Master Mariner, long a local hero, role model, and favorite son of Stonington, Connecticut.

Captain Palmer was arguably America's most accomplished and famous sailor of the first half of the nineteenth century; a fourteen-year-old crewman on a blockade runner in the War of 1812; discoverer of "Palmer Land" Antarctica in 1820 as captain of his own ship; a gun runner in the West Indies for Simon Bolivar's 1820s revolution against Spain; a captain of packet ships and clipper ships at the center of the booming transatlantic trade in the 1830s and 1840s; key inspiration in the 1840s for the design and building of the Houqua, one of the first and fastest Chinese tea clipper ships at the height of the last age of sail in 1844; and a founding member of the New York Yacht Club. Nathaniel was an early family friend of Captain Richard Loper, who sailed with him to Antarctica in 1820, designed the schooner Madgie in 1857, and later modified and renamed her Magic to become the first defender of the America's cup in 1870.

This story is woven from previous biographies of Captain Palmer and extensive previously unpublished correspondence with his wife, Eliza, and numerous sisters, brothers, nieces, nephews, brothers-in-law, and business associates contained both in the Palmer-Loper and Bradford-Fanning-Stanton family papers at the Stonington Historic Library, Library of Congress in Washington D.C., and other family archives.

This paints the picture of an adventurous and persuasive businessman, talented sea captain, loving husband, and family benefactor who spared no effort or expense to take care of those around him through a number of shipboard adventures and family tragedies. He earned much love and respect from his family and those who knew him, even though he was absent at sea much of the time.

Nathaniel had ancestral ties to the founding Brown family of Providence, Rhode Island, and to John Nicholas Brown, whose Newport family home, Harbor Court, is now the site of the New York Yacht club. Another Brown descendant was Nathaniel Herreshoff, whose accomplishments as a yacht and ship designer and builder dominated the American maritime scene in the decades prior to World War I. Herreshoff's name remains at the forefront of American Maritime History. Captain Nathaniel Palmer's name belongs there too.

—Rod Johnstone, Cofounder and Designer, J Boats, Inc., Newport, Rhode Island, and Stonington, Connecticut

PRINCIPAL CHARACTERS

PALMER-FANNING-BRADFORD-STANTON FAMILY MEMBERS

Nathaniel Brown Palmer (1799–1877), the nineteenth century sea captain from Stonington, Connecticut, is the subject of this book.

Eliza Babcock Palmer (1810–1872) was married at just sixteen to Nathaniel. They did not have children of their own.

Alexander Smith Palmer (1806–1894) was Nathaniel's younger brother by seven years. He followed his brother, becoming a noted ship captain.

Priscilla Dixon Palmer (1815–1851) was Alexander's loving wife who became Eliza's best friend. She and Alex had four children.

Nathaniel "Natty" Palmer II (1840–1877) was the oldest child of Alex and Priscilla. He was like a son to Uncle Nathaniel.

Juliet Palmer Fanning (1808–1845) was Nathaniel's sister. She married sea captain William Fanning, who died young and left her with their daughter, Sarah.

Sarah Fanning Bradford (1825–1919), a precocious young woman who wrote colorful journals detailing many trips with her Palmer-Stanton family members.

Joseph Warren Stanton (1800–1880) married Nathaniel's sister Grace (1802–1871), moved to New Orleans, and was the families' guide to this key southern port city where many family members worked and lived.

Edmund Fanning (1769–1841) was one of Stonington's noted early sea captains. He became a mentor to Nathaniel, was the father-in-law of Juliet, and supportive grandfather of Sarah.

NATHANIEL PALMER'S MARITIME SUPPORTERS

Russian Admiral Fabian von Bellinghausen (1788–1852) discovered

Antarctica in January 1820, ten months before Nathaniel sighted it.

Simon Bolivar (1783–1830) liberated five countries in northern South America from Spanish rule and employed Captain Palmer to run guns and soldiers for his activities throughout the West Indies.

Edward Knight Collins (1802–1878) was the major American player in the packet trade between England and the United States. Nathaniel became commodore of his fleet of packet ships.

Abbot A. Low (1811–1893) was the senior brother of the Low family from Salem and New York who became major ship owners and merchants with China. Captain Palmer became a partner in their firm.

Howqua Wu Bingjian, known as "Houqua" (1769–1843), a senior Chinese merchant who was given authority by the Chinese government to supervise all trading activities by western vessels in the Hong area specifically allocated to them near Canton on the Pearl River.

FAMILY TREES *of* PRINCIPAL CHARACTERS

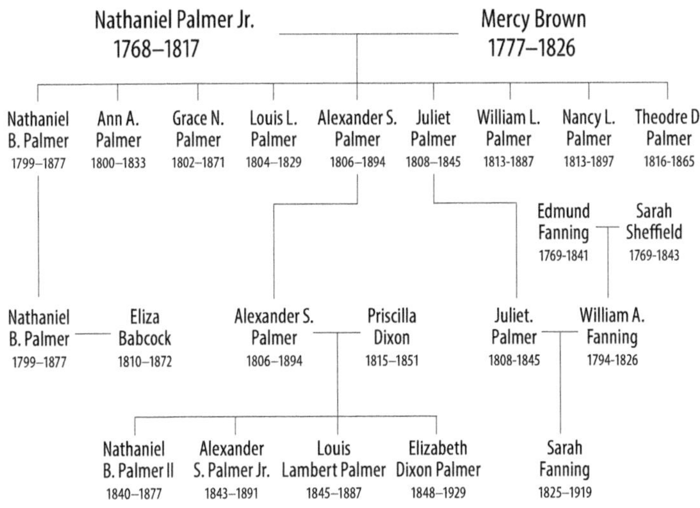

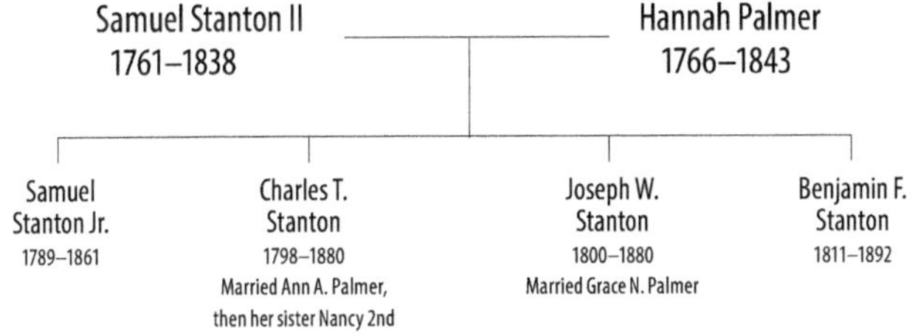

Family trees by Chelsea Mitchell

MAPS

PREVAILING TRADEWINDS

These winds are constant and reliable. They are created by the geography of the earth and the earth's orientation to the sun. In the days of sailing ships, they facilitated trade around the world.

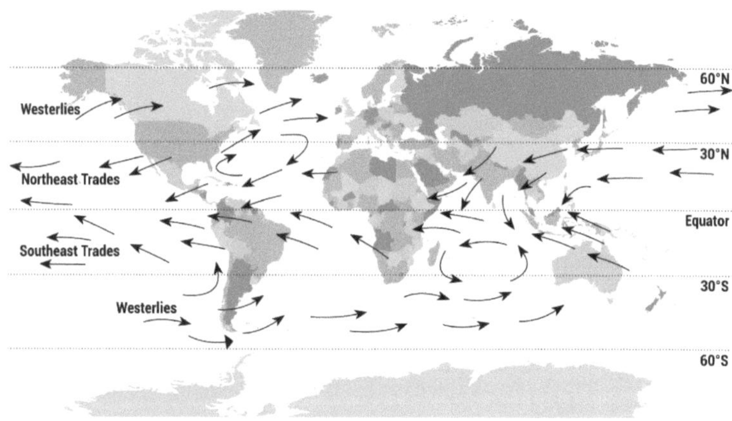

By Mark Scott & Chelsea Mitchell; Graphic Design, Sue Fornara

The Canton traders preferred to sail to and return from China via the Cape of Good Hope. The winds were more moderate and the sailing time quicker, although it was a longer distance than around Cape Horn. Cape Horn is more than 1,000 miles farther south than Cape of Good Hope, and at that latitude there is no other land to slow the westerly winds down—hence the "furious 50s." Better sailing rigs evolved, and by the time of the California gold rush, sailing ships could more efficiently sail through the westerlies around Cape Horn. From there they would work their way up to San Francisco, and then sail to China in the easterlies. They would return from China via Cape Horn and catch the westerlies.

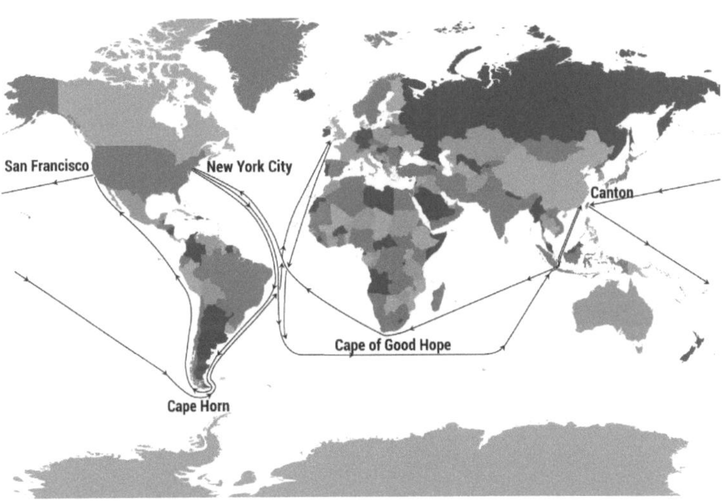

By Mark Scott & Chelsea Mitchell; Graphic Design, Sue Fornara

Nathaniel Palmer left Stonington on August 1, 1820, on his forty-seven-foot sloop *Hero*, reaching Captain Pendleton's sealing fleet in the South Shetlands in the autumn. Sent farther south into unknown territory to search for seals, on November 15 he reached Deception Island, entering her narrow harbor. Climbing to a high ridge, he looked across Bransfield Strait and sighted the northern edge of Antarctica, now named Palmer Land.

By Mark Scott & Chelsea Mitchell; Graphic Design, Sue Fornara

Within half a century from his birth in 1799, the borough Nathaniel grew up in changed dramatically. Local sea captains made fortunes in the sealing trade, and the introduction of the railroad in 1837 accelerated its progress. Shops, hotels, restaurants, and businesses sprang up, and many of the houses in Stonington Borough were built between 1820 and 1860. His birthplace is marked on this map.

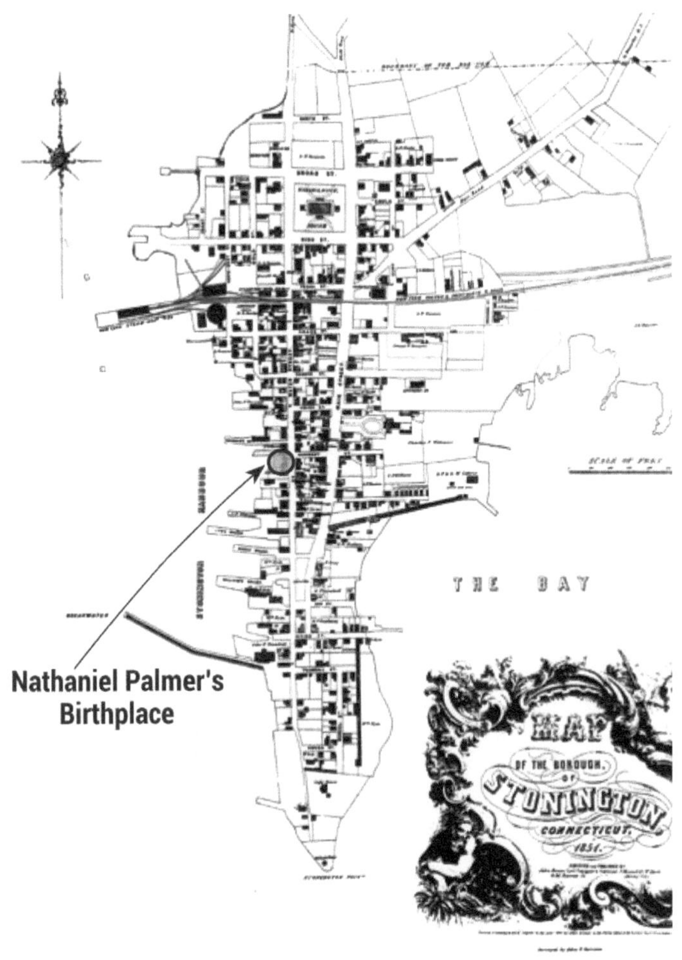

SHIPS GLOSSARY

By Mark Scott

Early wooden sailing ships from the seventeenth to the nineteenth century were constructed of wood, held together by iron fasteners, rigged with hemp rope, and powered by canvas sails. It was all about speed; faster was better in all cases. Although the various ships were built of the same materials, their designs could not be more different.

In the early to mid-nineteenth century, designers and builders understood more about hydrodynamics than aerodynamics, so one of the main differences was in the size and shape of the hull. There was no empirical data relating speed to sail area and hull shape. The amount of volume of a hold or storage below decks was easy to determine.

As ship building technology evolved, the hulls got bigger and the masts taller. We will look at a select number of ships that Captain Palmer sailed, focusing on their rigging type and the number of masts they carried.

SLOOPS

These ships had only a single mast and were limited in their size. Their main sail was trapezoidal in shape and ran fore and aft, with a boom on the bottom and a mini boom, the gaff, on top. This sail configuration required only a small crew to control. The hulls were typically narrow, forming a V, and were agile and easily driven.

Courtesy of Public Domain

Nathaniel Palmer sailed the forty-seven-foot sloop *Hero* down the Atlantic in 1820. The *Hero*'s fore and aft sail configuration allowed him to sail her with a crew of four because it took only two or three men to reef or furl the large main sail of a sloop. That same sail configuration allowed him to sail much closer to the wind, perhaps 45° off the wind. Square rigged sails do not allow you to sail much more than 70° to the wind.

For sailing in and out of shallow harbors, a light and easily maneuverable sloop was ideal. He left later for the West Indies on the sloop *James Monroe* and returned in record time, demonstrating a sloop could make profitable runs of 1,500–1,800 miles.

BRIGS, BRIGANTINES, and SCHOONERS

These ships had two masts. The fore mast was typically shorter than the aft, so the main sail(s) were on the aft mast. With the exception of the schooner, they were square rigged. We are referring to the direction of the sails relative to the centerline of the ship. Although the sails were rectilinear in shape, they were mounted from "yards" at right angles to the keel. These cross-arms could be pivoted at their midpoint to take advantage of the wind coming from the stern quarter. The real power came when the trade winds would blow from behind or on the beam, pushing the ship along its way.

Courtesy of Public Domain

The brig and brigantine hulls were flat and wide and could be used for carrying large cargoes of men and ammunition. They were hybrids and combined power and maneuverability. In 1824, Nathaniel sailed the schooner *Cadet* to Cartagena, Colombia. The trade winds in the Caribbean are strong easterlies and pile up a lot of water on the coast of Panama. A schooner rigged vessel, with its fore and aft sails, would have allowed Nathaniel to sail closer to the wind to get around Cuba and into the Gulf Stream.

Nathaniel then captained a brig, the *Tampico*. It was longer than the *Cadet*, carrying a wide beam all the way back to the stern, allowing it to carry more cargo. Its hybrid rig of fore and aft sails combined with square sails on its two masts and gave it both power and maneuverability. Later he made two passages around the Horn with a larger brig, the *Annawan*.

FULL-RIGGED SHIPS, BARQUES, and BARQUENTINES

These ships had three masts and mountains of sail. They could move bulky or heavy cargo quickly around the world. Ship-building technology was evolving in the mid-nineteenth century, and ships were getting bigger and faster. The packet ships Captain Palmer sailed across the Atlantic or along the east coast from New York to New Orleans were built broad and deep. Their hulls were nearly flat with a kettle-shaped hull. He returned from Liverpool in 1835 with ideas for creating a new generation of packet ships that would be larger and, with their new hull shape, faster. They carried towering masts with four courses of sail.

Courtesy of Public Domain

Captain Palmer inspired a new design for a class of boat in the China trade called a clipper. They would be bigger and leaner with more sail area than the packets. Their hulls would be more streamlined, and the ships would be faster than their predecessors, the packets. Their primary cargo would be tea shipped to England and America.

He inspired and captained the first American clipper, the *Houqua*. She was built as a fully rigged ship with three masts, and her hull had an extended concave bow above the water line with a fuller, flat-bottomed hull at her midsection and tapered at the stern. Her extensive sail plan, with five courses of sail on her main mast, was powerful. She was built for speed and endurance.

Courtesy of Andrey Chaikin

AUTHOR'S PREFACE

WHEN I STARTED THIS BOOK, I had no idea that studies of the greater Palmer-Loper-Fanning-Bradford-Stanton family journals and correspondence would result in three revealing discoveries about the New England Sea captains of the early-mid nineteenth century. First, whatever courage, skill, tenacity, and ingenuity Nathaniel Palmer and his brother Alexander required to reach their challenging objectives was more than shared by the superb wives and sisters who supported them. Wives Eliza and Priscilla and sister Juliet's leadership was outstanding. Second, their striking achievements might never have happened without the constant help they received from many other seafaring families in their community.

The family values of these early nineteenth-century families may have been even deeper than those we share today. The story of Nathaniel Brown Palmer's life is one of the women and intertwined families who empowered him, but it also reflects the family bonds forming his world. This generation of seafaring families who lived two hundred years ago appear to have lived by a deeper, less self-centered system of values than we enjoy today. The emphasis and driving force in their lives was "What is good for the family?" rather than "What is good for me?"

This latter motivation forms much of our twenty-first-century culture; the former family-oriented one created an environment in which everyone was concerned with developing and helping each other. The social media culture that has drawn in so many of our younger people may be responsible for this current move from "We" to "I." Let's all work to help our wonderful children and grandchildren gently move back to the "We" by recreating the old-fashioned values of the nineteenth-century Palmer-Loper-Fanning-Bradford-Stanton families we will become acquainted with in this book.

CHAPTER 1

NATHANIEL PALMER'S BOYHOOD
—STONINGTON, CONNECTICUT

NATHANIEL BROWN PALMER, born in Stonington, Connecticut, on August 8, 1799, bore the name of his grandfather (born in Stonington in 1740) and his father (born in 1768). The birthplace of these men was a small New England town on the Atlantic Ocean with a natural harbor at the eastern end of Long Island Sound. Many of its citizens were seafaring people. His mother, Mercy Brown from nearby Providence, Rhode Island, was from the Brown family of leading mariners; Brown University was named after them. His father, Nathaniel Palmer Jr., was a lawyer who also had a small shipyard on the harbor where young Nathaniel spent much of his youth.

His forebears had come to Stonington in the early 1600s. The first English settlers built their houses next to a saltwater cove they named for the local Indian tribe. Today a prominent sign there reads: 1650 Wequetequock Burial Ground — Stonington Founders Cemetery. A large stone column is inscribed with the names of some of Stonington's original families: Palmer, Stanton, Cheseborough, and Minor. Large six-by-two-foot granite slabs cover the earliest graves. They were called "wolfstones" since they protected the departed from being dug up by animals.

Firstborn Nathaniel Palmer had four brothers and five sisters, one of whom, Mercy, died in childbirth. Three of his four brothers- Alexander, William, and Theodore-became sea captains as well.

His four sisters married young men from the local Fanning and Stanton families who also were sea captains.

From boyhood on, Nathaniel was described and singled out first as a reliable boy and later as a highly dependable man who received immediate respect when he boarded a vessel as its captain. He grew into a powerful man who was over six feet tall with a commanding presence. He had the rare ability to inspire those who worked with-and later for-him with his confidence under pressure. By the time he shipped out at fourteen on a local blockade runner evading British warships that were trying to confine Stonington's trading fleet during the War of 1812, Nathaniel understood he would spend his life on the ocean.

Stonington Borough, where he was born, was a promontory of land two miles long and little more than half a mile wide jutting out into the Atlantic Ocean. It was then called "The Point." Facing across the Atlantic two miles from The Point was the east end of Fisher's Island. Nathaniel was born and brought up in a simple white colonial house at 94 Water Street, Stonington.

The house was owned by Peleg Brown, father of Nathaniel's mother, Mercy Brown. Nathaniel Palmer Jr. and his wife, Mercy, were living at 94 Water Street when Nathaniel was born. It was customary in those days for young couples to live with one of their parents until they could afford their own home.

The rear of the house faced west over Stonington's interior harbor, an anchorage safe from the frequent Nor'easter storms. Later, the men of Stonington would enhance the harbor's safety by building a breakwater protecting it from the Atlantic Ocean. The other eastern side of the long, narrow borough faced the Atlantic Ocean between it and Watch Hill, Rhode Island. Miles out into the Atlantic beyond Watch Hill was Block Island.

The Atlantic Ocean surrounding Stonington would provide its sea-faring families such as the Palmers with access to faraway countries and their sovereigns. Just after the turn of the nineteenth century, the Palmer family became distantly involved with Tsar-Emperor Alexander I of Russia. He was an exotic figure otherwise as inaccessible to these early American families as the

Chinese rulers of Canton they would later encounter in their role as mariners on the world's oceans.

Living at 94 Water Street in the Borough before and after Nathaniel's birth was an enslaved black servant who took the name Phyliss Brown after her master, Peleg Brown. Years before Phyliss had married Pero Hallam, a slave owned by two Stonington merchants who eventually gave him his freedom in 1801.

When Nathaniel Brown Palmer grew up in this town on the east coast of the United States and went to sea, many of the sailors on those Atlantic Ocean waters were black Americans. They will have an active role to play in this story of his life.

Phyliss and her husband, Pero, earlier had a daughter named Prudence. About 1807, Prudence married a freed black man named Claude Gabriel in Providence, Rhode Island. They had two children— a girl named Annetta and a boy named Saviere. In 1810, Claude shipped out from Providence as steward-cook on the American ship *President Adams* bound for St. Petersburg, Russia; it was captained by Richard Field.

By 1803, black men made up about 18 percent of the seamen employed on the Atlantic coast. Most of them were freemen. Going to sea was a good employment opportunity for many who preferred this to working on farms. Many became respected members of the churches and other societies in the free black communities in northern cities.[1]

While walking the streets of St. Petersburg off duty from his ship, Claude was sighted by the Tsar of Russia passing in his carriage. The Tsar wanted this tall, handsome black man to be part of his entourage and took him into his service in the palace against the wishes of the American captain of the *President Adams*. Claude became homesick for his wife and children in America and asked the Tsar if he could bring them to St. Petersburg.

John Quincy Adams was then the U.S. Ambassador to Russia. Adams's diary entry of August 13, 1811, reads: "Gave a passport to the Black man in the Emperor's service, Claude Gabriel, who is going to Providence R.I. to bring his wife and children back."

The Tsar ordered Claude to wear his fancy Russian dress uniform complete with a saber while in the United States, but since this led to severe physical attacks on him in the streets of Boston, he had to hide them away.[2]

Prudence Gabriel agreed to travel with her husband Claude to St. Petersburg with her children. Prudence, Annetta, and Savier were christened in a church in Providence on March 3, 1812. Just before their departure, Prudence wrote a moving letter to her mother, Phyliss Brown:

Providence, April 6, 1812

My dear Mother,

As I expect to board ship tomorrow to commence
my passage to St Petersburg in Russia, I cannot leave
without again expressing my great sorrow that it has
so happened that I shall never more behold my dear
Parents faces in this life…I shall endeavor to leave you
and trust to the Mercies of a kind heavenly Parent who
provides for and protects us all…I must beg of you to
write me at Russia as vessels every year in the Spring
sail there from Boston, Providence and New York.
Please direct them to Claude Gabriel at the Emperor's
Palace where they will get to my hand and gratify
me. And that the Almighty may continue his blessing
upon you and my honored Father [Pero Hallam].

Your Dutiful Daughter, Prudence Gabriel[3]

By the time Nathaniel Palmer was born in 1799, houses like his grandfather's in the Borough were simple white dwellings that later might be transformed into larger, more elegant Federal style houses. Sometimes two smaller buildings side by side in the early days would eventually be rebuilt as one larger dwelling to accommodate different generations. This occurred later when 94 and 96 Water Street became 94 as it is now. The most prominent of these houses were often owned by successful sea captains or investors in vessels following the profitable trade in fur seal skins obtained in voyages in the icy waters below Argentina.

One of the most prominent early sea captains from Stonington was Edmund Fanning. In the *Brig Betsy* from 1797–1799, Fanning sailed to the Falkland Islands off Argentina for fur seal skins, and then sailed south and west around the Horn into the Pacific Ocean, where he picked up more skins and sandalwood. He brought his cargo of more than 100,000 skins and precious wood to Canton China, where he sold it, making a handsome profit for himself and his investors.[4]

Like many boys born in these coastal towns, Nathaniel grew up admiring the sailors who came back to port with their fascinating stories of the sea. He learned to swim and loved the water as a child. He went to his father's shipyard after school, where he was encouraged by the returning sailors to climb the riggings, heard their tales, and explored their ships while dreaming of going to sea himself.

Nathaniel Palmer began to understand the basics of how ships were built from the various types of woods that were used by local shipyards. First were those that came from American forests. Southern live oak was the most valuable source of the structural part of vessels exposed to the water because of its resistance to the effects of salt water. Connecticut white oak, being coarse-grained and easily shaped, was the basic hardwood used for many purposes. Locally available rock maple was used for key components in parts of the ship underwater, such as the keel, because of its strength. Deck planking used the less expensive and easily available white pine. Finer woods for the interior cabins had to be brought in from afar and were much more expensive.[5]

The young man also began to observe and use the various tools required for shaping the different woods, such as the adze and saw. Various stands of trees were plentiful in America, and a ship carefully built from the right woods could last a long time. But since his father's shipyard was relatively small, his exposure to shipbuilding probably included visits to shipyards of family friends and neighbors where the larger vessels were built. This exposure as an impressionable child stood him in good stead when he creatively influenced the leading designers of larger ships so many years later.[6]

Boys in small New England ports such as Stonington did not go to sea out of necessity. They could become farmers or tradesmen, but many chose willingly to become sailors. They realized it was a rewarding activity that could lead to an exciting career. They might become a ship's mate or even a captain. Boys in these seafaring towns in the early nineteenth century were expected to become responsible men well before they reached the age of twenty.

These boys should not be compared to our sons or grandsons today in the twenty-first century, whose challenge at sixteen to twenty may be to decide what college subject to major in, what sport to play, what young lady to romance, or whether to attend graduate school. Nathaniel was brought up and expected to behave like a man well before our young men now reach that degree of competence and maturity.

Young Nathaniel observed that the best houses in Stonington were owned by successful ship captains. If he worked hard to become a skillful, dedicated mariner he might someday own one of them. Along the way, he hoped to persuade one of the desirable girls in Stonington or adjacent Westerly, Rhode Island, to marry him.

His family, the Palmers, and many of their closest Stonington friends, such as the Fannings, Stantons, and Lopers, were involved with the sea as ship captains, sailors, shipbuilders, dock owners, provisioners, and investors in various shipping activities. These families spent a great deal of time together at work and socially. Not surprisingly, many of their children married each other.

This small world at the edge of the Atlantic Ocean with its intermarriages and other relationships was very supportive for a young man such as Nathaniel, who wished to go to sea. He didn't have to ask a stranger for a job; one of his Stonington relatives or their friends would have him join their shipyard, learn to sail on one of their vessels, or work as a clerk in a related seafaring activity.

The key mariner families in New England's other seafaring towns helped each other both with wise counsel and investment. We will learn later in Nathaniel's story how the wealthy Low family of Salem and New York City became instrumental in his success in the clipper ship world.

In those early days, each New England seaport town had its own specialty. Marblehead concentrated on Grand Banks fishing, Salem on the China clipper trade, and New Bedford on sealing and whaling. Nearby Mystic's Greenman brothers built many of America's important large mid-nineteenth-century wooden vessels before they were overtaken by iron-hulled ships powered by steam. Nantucket became the greatest whaling port in the world until whale oil was replaced by oil pumped from the earth and then refined.

During the Revolutionary War, the British began a blockade of New England ports that led to countermeasures from the local American captains. These aggressive, privateering practices against British ships by colonial investors and sea captains from 1775 to 1783 were renewed by privateers from Stonington, Mystic, New London, and other Connecticut ports during the blockade of its trading vessels in the following War of 1812.[7]

American privateers during the Revolution and thereafter were subject to rules set up first by the Continental Congress during the Revolution and later by the U.S. Government or states during the War of 1812. Privateering American ships had to first procure a Privateer Commission and then abide by uniform rules of conduct supervised by Prize Courts established to authorize the seizure and distribution of privateer prize proceeds from the ships captured with their cargos. Privateers sometimes had to post monetary bonds.[8]

British ships were not the only vessels often seriously short of crew. Stonington ship captains and their first mates also impressed their American brothers into service. There is a story of two unfortunate American seamen in 1814 who became drunk one night in a nearby New London, Connecticut, grog shop. They awakened the next morning aboard a Stonington ship sailing to distant waters.[9]

Both Stonington shipowners and sailors understood the risks of having either their ships or bodies seized by the British or even by a neighbor. Ship owners therefore bought and sold their unarmed ships and privateers in thirty-two shares so they were never too concentrated in ownership of one vessel. By also investing in privateers, they ensured they could take back some of the interests they might lose when their own ships were seized by foreign privateers.

Usually several wealthy investors owned the majority of a ship's shares with the rest split into smaller lots. Keeping their ships from being captured required hiring the ablest, most daring sailors as captains. These captains were well paid and were given shares in the vessels they commanded as partial compensation. They often became wealthy men and meaningful ship owners themselves. Nathaniel began to receive modest ownership shares in vessels after his initial voyages.[10]

As the war between France and England went on from 1799 to 1815, many British sailors were attracted to transferring to American ships, lured by better treatment and higher pay. They were also encouraged to become naturalized American citizens. It is estimated that as many as several thousand did so. This enraged the British Navy, which had trouble finding enough men to man their huge ocean fleets during their sixteen-year war against Napoleon.

They began to board the American maritime fleet to seize any seaman they thought was a British subject, regardless of his current situation. The American captains could not protect their sailors from these actions by powerful British well-armed navy vessels. The Royal Navy became more aggressive as their need for seamen increased, and they often ignored the American claims that many seamen they seized either had become American citizens or originally were Americans. They were also capable of seizing sailors while on shore from their ships.

The number of sailors needed to crew British ships went from 36,000 in 1793 to 114,000 in 1812. Conditions on these ships could be brutal and cruel. It was estimated that as many as 100,000 Royal Navy service men died during that twenty-year period. British Lord Horatio Nelson said, "Without a press, I have no idea how our Fleet can be manned."[11]

The British Navy simply took a seaman from his American ship and put him on a British ship where he could be forced to serve for years under the control of the British captain. The impressed sailors could be moved from one British ship to another when it served their captors' needs. They were watched carefully in port to prevent them from escaping. Despite that, some were able to do so and eventually made their way back to the United States. This was the case of Jeremiah Holmes from Mystic, Connecticut, whom we will soon meet.

During Britain's wars with Napoleon, the British impressed up to ten thousand sailors actually born in the United States. In June 1812, the American government declared war on England, even though its Navy was no match either for the British Royal Navy or its large merchant privateers. The Americans also considered attacking Canada. The British considered the Americans a nuisance before the War of 1812. Their major concern through the early 1800s was winning or ending their longer, much more important war with Napoleon, waged from 1799 to 1815.[12]

CHAPTER 2

WAR *of* 1812—YOUNG BLOCKADE RUNNER *and* SEALER *in the* SOUTHERN SEAS

THIS WAS THE SITUATION when Nathaniel Brown Palmer first went to sea at age fourteen in 1814 on a Stonington blockade runner. Many of the New England blockade runners trying to evade British warships and privateers in the War of 1812 were concentrated in Stonington or nearby New London. One of the favorite haunts of the British warships hunting them was the Fishers Island Sound waters between Fishers Island and Stonington on the nearby Connecticut coast, and the Atlantic Ocean waters eastward of Stonington along the adjacent Rhode Island coast past Watch Hill.

Nathaniel Palmer shipped out as an ordinary seaman on the blockade-running sloop *Fortune*, which ran various goods in and out of Boston and New York City harbors. He learned to pay attention to the sounds waves make in various shallow waters to determine how close to shore his ship could safely sail. The blockade runners did this to avoid the larger British warships that couldn't come in that close. These early challenging sailing experiences prepared Nathaniel to deal with the awesome winds, tides, bad weather, crew disturbances, ice flows, and other risks he would encounter years later sailing in the icy southern fur sealing seas around the South Pole.

Here is an example of one of Nathaniel Palmer's cruises on the *Fortune*. It was coming back to Stonington from Boston, sailing southwest along the Rhode Island coast off Weekapaug just east of Watch Hill and several miles east of Stonington Harbor. Nathaniel was the first to sight a British frigate. He said to his master, Captain Dennis: "It's the *Eolus*, sir. She's seen us." Captain Dennis knew the British ship was well armed, faster than his vessel, and could easily capture them in navigable waters. The *Eolus* began to shell them with round shot off their bow and stern. He took his ship close to shore by Watch Hill reef, racing for the shoal water inside Gangway Rock. Before the *Eolus* could intercept him, Captain Dennis managed to run the last obstacle between his ship and the safety of Stonington harbor, now just two miles away around Napatree Point. Only bold, clever seamanship and an intimate knowledge of local waters saved his ship.[1]

The ships Nathaniel served on left port at night or in heavy fog or storm to avoid the blockading English ships in the War of 1812. They sailed to major northern Atlantic ports to pick up cargo such as salted fish, grain, or livestock, then down to the American southern ports and the West Indies to deliver their cargo. While there, they bought sugar, rum, rice and flour, luxury goods from Europe, and cotton for northern mills. They then brought these goods back for their customers in the northern states. Their survival required constant vigilance. They were at risk when the fog lifted because they could be seen by the vigilant British ships watching for them.

Nathaniel was at sea on a blockade runner when the most momentous event in Stonington's history occurred. On the afternoon of August 9, 1814, the small port town was ordered to evacuate by a powerful squadron of British warships claiming the Village of Stonington had furnished torpedoes to American ships attacking the British fleet in Long Island waters. The townspeople refused, and the four British ships began bombarding Stonington with cannon fire that damaged many dwellings but miraculously did not directly kill any inhabitants.

Nathaniel's boyhood friend Richard Loper made a much-needed discovery. Richard found kegs of gunpowder lying hidden beside the States Pottery factory near the sea on Stonington Point.

This proved to be invaluable in helping the Stonington men make cartridges for their two eighteen-pounders and one brass six-pounder cannon. This was their total armament against the British men of war. Six years later in 1820, Richard would serve on the crew of Nathaniel's sloop *Hero* in its journey to Antarctica.

Over the next four days, British warships with 160 cannons and 1,275 officers and men bombarded the town with fifty tons of cannon balls and made several assaults on its beaches. All of these were repulsed by the local men. Stonington was successfully defended by only its three cannons, the 13th Regiment of Militia, and local Stonington men.

In retrospect, the relatively minor damages suffered by dwellings in Stonington and the relative lack of serious injury or deaths seems almost miraculous considering the favored advantages and firepower enjoyed by the British fleet besieging the little town. Only a few locals and militia were injured, and no one was killed. Only four houses were destroyed and another thirty or forty damaged.[2]

The Stonington defense effort and its cannon crews were led by Captain Jeremiah Holmes, an American sailor who previously had been trained as an expert gunner by the British Navy. He had been impressed into the Royal Navy for three years and finally managed to escape in 1807 after several attempts to return to America. Holmes then settled in Mystic, Connecticut, just west of Stonington.

The year before the British attacked Stonington, Holmes had been captain and one-quarter owner of the sloop *Hero*, a sound well-constructed coaster built in Mystic, Connecticut, in 1800. Early in 1813, he had taken her down the coast to Virginia where he picked up flour, which he later sold in Boston, and then farther down the Atlantic coast to Charleston for rice, which he sold in Philadelphia. Both transactions would bring him enormous profits.

During his journey, Captain Holmes was warned that the British Navy had undertaken a dangerous blockade of the American Atlantic coast. Undeterred by the enormous risks involved, Holmes continued his voyage. He narrowly avoided being taken or sunk by British ships of the line. He would have been seized by a British privateer, but at the last moment the ship allowed him to escape to capture a larger American prize, the *Ulysses*, which it sank after taking its cargo and men.[3]

This same sloop *Hero* was the vessel commanded by twenty-one-year-old Nathaniel Palmer six years later when he took her down the Atlantic Ocean to "discover" Antarctica.

The British fleet attacking Stonington was commanded by Captain Hardy, the same man who stood beside Admiral Nelson during the battle of Trafalgar when Nelson was shot by a Spanish sniper and famously said: "Kiss me, Hardy. I am dying." The British suffered twenty-one dead and fifty wounded during the Battle of Stonington. This was one of the most impressive American victories ever over another nation's superior force.

After the War of 1812 with England ended in late December 1814, the United States assisted mariners such as the Stonington ship captains by protecting their trading rights along the Atlantic coast. The Tariff of 1816 prohibited foreign vessels from delivering woolen and other cloth to America. Other coastal shipping laws were enacted that protected American trading vessels from foreign competition.[4]

The impression and/or imprisonment of thousands of American sailors by the Royal Navy during the Napoleonic wars against Europe and England from 1799–1815 had led the new United States to declare war against England in 1812. Seventy percent of the seamen sent to prison had been captured by British ships while serving on American privateers. Few had been American Navy personnel, and like many sailors on privateers, they often came from the bottom of society. They had virtually no one who would represent or protect them when they were captured by the British.

Since the capture of American ships and their crews by the British before and during the War of 1812 was such a key factor in forming the experience of many American sailors when Nathaniel Palmer first went to sea, we will examine the fate of the thousands of American sailors sent to Dartmoor Prison in England when they were seized on American ships from 1813 to 1815.

When the American War of 1812 was ended by the Peace Treaty of Ghent on Christmas Eve 1814, many of the captured American sailors were in England's Dartmoor Prison, built to handle Britain's prisoners from overseas. It was situated on a lonely moor in Southwest England and had been opened in 1809. It became the largest, most feared prison in the vast world of detention facilities the British created to contain prisoners from its far-flung empire. It could hold up to 10,000 prisoners.

Many French prisoners from the Napoleonic wars with Britain from 1799 to 1814 were being held there as well. The British began to release all their French prisoners from Dartmoor when their conflict with France ended in late December 1814. At that time, American prisoners of war were still being held and transferred there from British overseas prisons in India, the Caribbean, Canada, and other dominions.

Nathaniel Palmer's cousin, Benjamin F. Palmer, born six years before him in 1793 as the son of Amos Palmer, was one of the Stonington privateering sailors who ended up in Dartmoor Prison. This quotation from the preface to Benjamin's diary demonstrates the challenges America's seamen faced in finding employment in the early 1800s when Nathaniel Palmer was growing up. Often the only way avid American sailors such as his cousin Benjamin could go to sea was on privateers.

> Under the operations of the "Orders in Council"
> of 1806, our merchant marine had been harassed
> and gradually driven from the sea, and the sailor
> stranded on shore. There were thousands of these
> men, perhaps the finest seamen the world ever
> knew, anxious to serve at sea but how. The regular
> Navy could take but a few, and it was left obviously
> for private enterprise to best find employment
> for this host of mighty men in two ways: 1) in
> letters of marque…vessels whose primary object is
> commerce…but also have guns and a commission
> from the [American] government to make prizes

[privateers]. Without such authorization, capture is
piracy. 2) Privateers owned, controlled, and manned
by a maritime people debarred from every other form
of maritime activity...[5]

To the horror of the 6,500 American prisoners at Dartmoor, most of them were not immediately released early in 1815 by the British when the War of 1812 was over. There were a few exceptions, such as Americans who had been officers on their ships or others who were freed at that time. However, James Madison, president of the United States from 1801 to 1817, was not interested in creating any more problems with the British. The American government basically ignored the plight of the great majority of their seamen remaining in Dartmoor.[6]

The American prisoners captured by the British on American privateers had the lowest priority to be released, ranking below naval officers, petty officers, and sailors seized on other countries' naval vessels. Many of their ships had come out of Stonington itself or nearby communities such as New London, Connecticut, only to be captured by the larger, better armed, faster, more powerful British privateers and the Royal Navy.[7]

About one thousand of the first American group of prisoners brought to Dartmoor were men of color. Soon after they began to arrive in Dartmoor in 1813, their white American counterparts asked their British guards to put the black fellow Americans into a separate compound rather than be associated with them as fellow prisoners. The American black sailors were all either ordinary seamen, cooks, or cabin boys. None were officers. That could only happen for them in the rare cases where the entire crew of an American ship was black.

The prison's governor, or "agent," Thomas Shortland, a former Royal Navy Captain, put the black American sailors in a separate prison block at Dartmoor. This was not the practice aboard ships, where white and black seamen slept together in bunk rooms below deck and ate together in the common mess.

They were all subject to the same common severe discipline from their vessel's Captain and his officers as well.

The discrimination and segregation black Americans endured during and after the American Civil War from 1861 to 1865 was initiated decades earlier when their white fellow American seamen in Dartmoor Prison insisted they be housed in a separate block. This block had more primitive conditions than the prison's other blocks where the rest of the prisoners were held. Dartmoor became the first prison where U.S. inmates were segregated. Outside Dartmoor prison today are the graves of the 271 Americans who died while in captivity there.

Although Ministers from England and the United States signed a Peace Treaty ending the War of 1812 on Christmas Eve 1814 in Ghent, sending copies to be ratified by each nation, many of the American prisoners were held in bad conditions at Dartmoor for months afterward without being released. Indeed, a horrible massacre of American prisoners occurred after a scuffle between the men and their British guards on April 6, 1815, over three months after the Peace Treaty was signed. Nine American prisoners were killed by the guards using their muskets, bayonets, and swords, and two dozen were seriously wounded. While Benjamin Palmer was finally released on April 27, 1815, other American prisoners waited even longer to be freed.[8]

Nathaniel Palmer's next significant experience at sea several years later indicated to interested sea captains and investors that this young man was destined to be an important captain himself one day. In 1819, when only eighteen, he shipped out of Stonington as second mate on the large two-masted brig *Hersilia*, captained by James Sheffield. Its voyage was financed by Captain Edmund Fanning. He had become rich by sealing and retired from the sea but now invested in sealing expeditions.

Sealing could be a nasty, risky activity. Masses of the large fur seals congregated on rock shelves jutting out over the water along the shores of islands and land masses in the icy southern waters. These seas were filled with dangerous ice floes, ice masses, high waves, risky tides, and other conditions presenting danger for the sealers. When the sailors jumped off their whale boats to these slippery rookeries—as the fur seal platforms were called—they sometimes fell to their deaths in the freezing waters. They soon learned how difficult it could be for their comrades to rescue them.[9]

Curiously, the sailors were not at risk from the large fur seals themselves, who idly watched as their brethren were clubbed to death by the eager sealers. Murdering and skinning their helpless prey was gruesome work. First the crewman would kill the seal with a blow to the head from a heavy club he carried. Then he had the bloody job of skinning the seals with a sharp knife on icy rocks covered with the seals' blood. The men learned to be extremely careful before attacking the much larger elephant blubber seals for their oil. These giant animals were capable of immediately knocking over any seaman who threatened their flocks of females and infants.

The first known sealing expedition from America was the *United States* sailing from Boston in 1784 to the Falkland Islands off southern Argentina. Its original objective was elephant seal oil. On arrival, the captain noticed the abundant fur seals in their rookeries and decided to harvest them instead. When he arrived back in Boston with 13,000 skins, they only brought fifty cents apiece. The buyer there sent them on to Calcutta, India. Several years later, another purchaser sent the same fur seal skins on to the market in Canton, China, where they finally fetched the fine price of $5 dollars apiece. American ships in Canton brought home the news of that profitable sale. The race for seal skins to sell to the Chinese market began, illustrating the volatility of pricing various goods could bring in different parts of the world in those early days.[10]

The search for profitable fur seal skins began in earnest. Over the next forty years until the late 1820s, sealers virtually exterminated most of the world's fur seals by slaughtering their huge, clustered families without remorse. It is estimated that the sealers from various countries killed more than 300,000 adults and 100,000 pups in the hunting seasons from 1820 to 1822.[11]

In 1819 when Edmund Fanning sent the *Hersilia* after seals with Nathaniel as its second mate, it reached former good sealing grounds in the Falkland Islands just off Argentina. Captain James Sheffield found the seal colonies there had been wiped out. Nathaniel had already been recognized as a lad of only eighteen who could handle special challenges. He was assigned by Sheffield to manage the animal stock and vegetable provisioning for ships, which had been developing in the Falkland Islands. Soon a large British ship, the *Espirito Santo*, arrived from Argentina for provisioning on the way to its sealing efforts in the South Shetland Islands. Nathaniel arranged to have the *Espirito Santo* provisioned with meat and vegetables from the Falklands. During this process, he also got to know its British Captain. This later helped the young man discern the *Espirito Santo*'s eventual destination.

The *Espirito Santo* was headed to the South Shetlands for seals. These islands were several hundred miles south of the Falkland Islands and just north of Antarctica. British Captain William Smith had previously discovered the South Shetlands in February 1819, but American sealers did not yet know of their existence. Instead, American sailors gave these islands they believed to be below the Falklands a romantic designation—"The Auroras."

When Nathaniel asked the British Captain where they were going, he received no answer; the captain had no intention of telling his American competitors where seals were still abundant for the taking. Nathaniel had the insight and zeal to use his compass, chart, and glass to observe and chart the course of the British ship leaving for the south from a high point on the Falklands. He may have even rushed to the shore to follow it secretly for a short distance in one of *Hersilia*'s small boats to better understand its course. He had befriended several of its crew members during provisioning who gave him additional information regarding their destination. Nathaniel then fully informed his superior, Captain James Sheffield, of his findings.[12]

Captain Sheffield took his ship down the course Nathaniel Palmer estimated the British ship had taken. When the Americans reached the South Shetlands and discovered the *Espirito Santo* actively sealing, its British Captain graciously shouted to them: "Never mind there are plenty of seal skins for all." This became the most southern point any Stonington sealing vessels had reached so far.[13]

The *Hersilia* returned to Stonington with an abundant cargo of fur seal skins sold to dealers there who would resell them in overseas markets. It had been a highly successful voyage for its owner and its crew. Young Nathaniel's share of the cargo was probably one in thirty-two or about 280 skins, which would sell for $560. This was a considerable sum in those days for a voyage lasting eight or nine months. He was beginning to come into his own as a young sailor destined to be entrusted with duties of increasing importance on his subsequent voyages.

During his next sealing voyage to the cold southern waters below Argentina, Nathaniel would be credited with the most important "discovery" of his life when he was only twenty-one years old.

CHAPTER 3

WHO DISCOVERED ANTARCTICA?

Nathaniel Brown Palmer's second voyage to the South Shetland Islands just above the ice-covered continent of Antarctica began August 1, 1820. He was only twenty and had just been appointed captain of the forty-seven-foot, four-crew sloop *Hero*. He sailed it alone without the protection and leadership of accompanying vessels. It took him more than three months to sail 10,000 miles south down the Atlantic Ocean past Argentina to meet with Captain Benjamin Pendleton's flotilla of eight Stonington ships that were then sealing in the South Shetland Islands.

When young Captain Palmer made his solo trip, the art of navigation was in a period of transition. On a long journey like his down the open sea, all the usual methods of coastal piloting such as depth findings and land sightings were not available. Finding north-south vertical latitude was not the prime challenge then. Sailors realized they could measure their latitude by observing the angle over the horizon of various celestial bodies, such as the North Star. By the fifteenth century, there were tables to calculate the sun's movement and increasingly sophisticated instruments to measure it and its angle over the horizon. Finding latitude was therefore no great challenge for him as he undertook his long trek south.[1]

The real challenge was how a sailor could find his east-west horizontal longitude far out at sea. The earth is a sphere of 360 degrees, and the sun rotates around it every twenty-four hours.

Each hour accounts for 15 degrees of rotation or longitude, and each degree four minutes.

If a sailor could determine the exact time at his ship's location and compare it to a separate fixed location (Greenwich, England's Prime Meridian Time), the difference was his longitude. But how could that sailor in 1820 accurately determine the time? This was required to make his longitude finding.

This failure to accurately determine time, and therefore longitude, had led British Admiral Sir Cloudesley Shovell in 1707 to run five ships under his command aground in the Isles of Scilly, causing the deaths of thousands of seamen when he was returning to England after his victorious conquest of Toulon. This inspired the British Parliament to enact the Longitude Act of 1714, which led to the development of an accurate portable clock by John Harrison in 1759. This was the predecessor to the modern chronometer.[2] The chronometer allowed mariners to accurately tell time at sea to determine their longitude. Astronomers had also been developing tables to calculate lunars, a more complex system for sailors to determine accurate time by observing the relation of the moon to the stars. These tables were used until World War I.

However, when Captain Palmer set out from Stonington in August 1820, chronometers were too expensive and even larger American merchant ships would not have had one. This is clear reading Richard Henry Dana's *Two Years Before the Mast*.[3] Calculating lunars was a highly complex process probably beyond Nathaniel's ability. So how did the young man sail down 10,000 miles of the open Atlantic staying on course to reach the distant South Shetland Islands only recently discovered by the Americans the previous year?

The *Hero's* log from his long voyage indicates that he used another, perhaps less exact but still serviceable, method to navigate longitude known as "Plaine Sailing." The term Plaine Sailing may refer to its simplicity or to the fact that it relied on the geometry of a right plane triangle. It required a mariner to first establish his latitude by dead reckoning corrected by celestial observation then to compare it to his last position. Each minute of latitude is a nautical mile. The difference in latitudes gave Nathaniel his progress north or south. This gave him the first leg of the triangle he would eventually need to determine his longitude or east-west horizontal position.

Next Nathaniel Palmer would estimate the distance and course he had run since his last position, using the compass course he was steering and the distance through the sea his log gave him. He would then apply a seaman's judgment regarding the effect of currents and wind on both his course steered and distance traveled. This calculation gave him the hypotenuse of his triangle.

He now only needed the remaining leg of the triangle. This would give him a fair estimate of his progress east or west in the Atlantic. Books available to him at that time would give him tables providing necessary calculations of compass degree. He would measure a mile of distance out to a few hundred miles, as well as the number of degrees of change of latitude. This gave him the remaining leg of his triangle.

For his 1820 voyage, Palmer used a helpful preprinted logbook titled *The Seaman's Journal: Being an Easy and Correct Method of Keeping the Daily Reckoning of a Ship During the Course of Her Voyage*.[4] Each page provided the spaces required to record the information needed by a mariner to calculate his position by Plaine Sailing. This process obviously worked for Nathaniel since he found his Stonington flotilla of ships in the South Shetlands. He also may have used Nathaniel Bowditch's leading guide for sailors of that time: *The American Practical Navigator*, 1779.[5]

Once down in the Southern Oceans, his navigation was probably made by dead reckoning, as the *Hero* felt her way among the islands and along what eventually proved to be the east coast of Antarctica. Nathaniel Palmer's log entry for November 1820 recording his entry into Deception Island's interior bay gives the latitude but no longitude, indicating that he used the Plaine Sailing method.[6]

Captain Nathaniel Palmer reached his Stonington sealing fleet in the South Shetlands on schedule in the autumn of 1820. Given his recent performance as second mate on the *Hersilia*, it is not surprising that Captain Pendleton decided to use his relatively small, agile sloop *Hero* as a search vessel for the fleet, since Nathaniel was also known to have unusually keen far-sighting ability. Pendleton instructed him to sail well south of the Shetlands to search for new rich seal rookeries.

Nathaniel followed his leader's orders and sailed south of the Shetlands to a site to be called Deception Island. He discovered it had a narrow opening. When he entered its harbor on November 15, 1820, he found hot springs and sandy beaches. This would later be named Yankee Harbor and become an ideal, safe haven for many American sealers. He climbed to the top of a high ridge on its edge and looked southwest across what would later be called Bransfield Straight after a British sealer-explorer who was there a year before in 1819.

Nathaniel Palmer saw what appeared to be a mountainous land mass across the ice-filled straight of water. The young captain of the *Hero* did not appreciate he had sighted the north peninsula coast of the continent of Antarctica. Eventually it would be designated "Palmer Land."

When he tried to sail to the perceived land mass across Bransfield Strait in the next few days, Nathaniel found the seas were full of sheets of moving ice and icebergs that prevented him from proceeding. He did not believe there were seals on this landscape, so he did not attempt to land on it. He returned to Deception Island and failed to make any indication in his log that he had just sighted Antarctica.[7]

Another source claims Nathaniel sighted Antarctica on November 16, 1820, while sailing on the *Hero* from Deception Island across the Bransfield Straight.[8] Still another claimed he discovered the continent two months later on January 14, 1821, sailing the *Hero* in the same waters.[9]

Several months later in early February 1821, Nathaniel Palmer returned to these same waters south and west of Deception Island. When he sounded the midnight bell, he was astonished to hear another ship's bell answer it. The next morning, the *Hero*'s crew was surprised to hear other voices. The fog lifted, and the men saw two large, splendid warships. They turned out to be Russian naval ships whose Captain Fabien Gottlieg von Bellinghausen invited him on board his ship the *Rostock* to meet his officers.

Nathaniel told the story of that meeting to Frederick Bush, the U.S. counsel in Hong Kong some twenty years later. His friends and supporters also spread what may have been a tale they embellished themselves, because Nathaniel Palmer was, and would be known throughout his career, as a man of integrity. The story that grew with the telling was printed many years later on January 28, 1907, in the *New London Globe* newspaper. It went unchallenged for 124 years during which the world's shipping community believed that twenty-one-year-old Captain Palmer on his forty seven foot sloop *Hero* discovered the great continent.

This is the much repeated version of the celebrated meeting between Bellinghausen and Palmer:

> Captain Bellinghausen dressed in his official Russian
> naval uniform, invites young Captain Palmer,
> dressed in seal skins, to meet with his elegant officers
> in his command cabin. "Be seated, young man.
> What are you doing here?" Palmer answers: "On a
> sealing expedition Sir." He then goes to get his ship's
> log to explain the details of the point where the *Hero*
> sights land and then describes to Bellinghausen
> specifics of the land he has recently sighted.
> After examining the *Hero's* log book and charts and
> discussing it with his officers, Captain Bellinghausen
> allegedly says: "What do I hear from a boy just out
> of his teens, commander of a small boat the size of
> the launch of my Frigate. He has pushed his way to
> the South Pole through ice. Then he has found the
> objective I have been searching for day and night for
> two weary years for my august master the Tsar of
> Russia. What shall I say to my master? Noble boy,
> wear your laurels with my sincere prayers. I name
> Palmer Land the place you have discovered."[10]

However, in the original handwritten report written by U.S. Counsel F.T. Bush in Hong Kong in the early 1840s and sent to D. Manning, U.S. Secretary of the Treasury, Bush describes the Russian who met with Nathaniel on board his ship in January 1821 as Admiral Kristerrstein, not Bellinghausen. Time had obviously affected the accuracy of this fabled story.[11]

The world finally learned that Captain Bellinghausen had clearly sighted the great continent about one year earlier in January 1820 when he was in these same waters with his ships. Bellinghausen had made detailed, specific reports of sighting mountains and other identifiable areas on Antarctica's land mass early in January 1820.

When Russian and world experts later carefully studied these reports, it became clear to all concerned that Bellinghausen earned the prize of being the first to discover Antarctica.[12]

Neither Bellinghausen, who had first sighted the peninsula jutting out from Northwest Antarctica in January 1820, nor Palmer who had first sighted the area ten months later in November of that year, actually set foot on the great continent as part of their discovery. Ironically, neither man understood what he had "discovered" when he did. Bellinghausen was searching for Antarctica to bring honor to his master, the Tsar of Russia, while Nathaniel Palmer was merely looking for seals.

But why didn't the world learn of this many years earlier, shortly after Bellinghausen returned to Russia after his three-year voyage to the South Pole in 1822 to render his findings? In the mid-1820s Russia was going through a revolt of young officers, which distracted government officials. Bellinghausen's reports, which only mentioned Nathaniel Palmer as a young American sailor, not as the discoverer of Antarctica, were basically ignored. When his reports were finally examined in detail years later, they determined that the great discovery of Antarctica was made by Captain Bellinghausen. However, even more time passed before this important conclusion was finally shared with the world maritime community. This dramatic, unexpected result only became fully available and translated into English in London in 1945, 124 years later!

As late as 1939, The American Philosophical Society issued a long report backing Dr. William Hobb's earlier finding that Nathaniel discovered Antarctica.[13] That conclusion was seconded in a special report of *United States Geographical Review* by Lawrence Martin of the Library of Congress.[14] The Americans continued to assert Captain Palmer's discovery without giving other claimants adequate consideration.

As suggested earlier, there is a third legitimate claim to the discovery of the great continent. British Captain Edward Bransfield probably sighted Antarctica on his ship *Williams* on January 30, 1820, just three days after Bellinghausen's discovery.

By the 1950s, seven countries had laid claim to one portion of Antarctica or another: Argentina, Australia, Chile, France, New Zealand, Norway, and the United Kingdom. No one nation claimed sovereignty to all of it, and none of them was particularly zealous about trying to enforce their smaller claims. Maps of the continent are covered by names of many sailors and explorers from various nations who had "discovered" its numerous bays, inlets, mountains, shelf and ice masses, and other locations. Interestingly, neither the United States nor Russia made a meaningful claim to it.

In 1959, the United States invited twelve countries with interest in the continent to a session in Washington, D.C. to establish a series of laws governing its use. Its key conditions were that human activity there be restricted to peaceful uses and that scientific cooperation between interested nations should continue. Membership in that agreement now includes fifty countries that contain 80 percent of the world's population.[15]

This fifth largest continent is not permanently populated because it is covered by vast, deep ice sheets sometimes two miles thick covering 5.4 million miles of mountain ranges, valleys, and plateaus that contain 60 percent of the world's fresh water. It took 45 million years to amass this ice sheet, which is now gradually being melted by climate change.

Two hundred years after its discovery a number of countries now have some form of government station in Antarctica monitoring the weather or other matters on the great continent. It is also continually being visited by a growing number of upscale tourist cruises and expeditions admiring its penguins, seals, other wildlife, and dramatic scenery of ice-covered mountains and valleys.

International tourists now avidly visit the early land mass exploration sites first established despite the daunting hardships endured by Antarctica's celebrated, intrepid explorers. They include: Robert Scott (1868–1912), Roald Amundson (1872–1928), Sir Ernest Shackleton (1874–1922), and Richard Byrd (1888–1957). A special trip to Antarctica, including champagne service from an elite ice bar, chef-prepared meals, and travel by private jet to and from the fabled continent became available in recent years to wealthy tourists. In 2023 its cost was $100,000 for a couple going for a full week.[16]

We close this saga of discoveries with a different one demonstrating how two sealers from different nations could cooperate as discoverers. In the next summer season of 1821–1822, George Powell, an Englishman several years older than Nathaniel Palmer, captained his scout ship the *Dove* back to the south seas looking for seals. Nathaniel Palmer, now captain of the larger sloop *James Monroe*, had returned for the same reason. Both young men soon discovered the fur seals were continually being depleted, although Powell eventually returned with a fair harvest.

The Englishman suggested they look for new rookeries farther east of the South Shetlands together, since a two-ship voyage would be safer. Sealers from different countries often helped each other survive the difficult conditions in these icy waters where storms could leave a group of their men stranded on a beach or cove for weeks.

On December 6, 1821, one of Powell's men sighted a group of four small ice-covered mountains 200 miles east of the South Shetlands. Captains Palmer and Powell sailed together to the largest one. They went ashore on the largest island to celebrate their discovery—the South Orkney Islands. They were less fortunate as sealers since few were there for the taking. Powell was more interested in the discovery than Palmer, who allowed him to make the first charts of the area, published later in London, and to claim the archipelago for Great Britain. As a young mariner or later as a mature one, Nathaniel Palmer was never anxious to seek credit for himself.[17]

CHAPTER 4

CARIBBEAN CHALLENGES—SAILING *for* SIMON BOLIVAR *and* EXPLORATION

CAPTAIN NATHANIEL BROWN PALMER's sealing efforts in the "south polar summer season" of 1821–1822 were unsuccessful even though he was involved with the co-discovery of the South Orkney Islands. He began to understand that the gradual extermination of fur seals in southern waters off South American was eliminating that key source of revenue. Further sealing would require journeying beyond Cape Horn to the Pacific Ocean as part of the Stonington fleet.

On January 25, 1822, his orders to return home from Captain Benjamin Pendleton, commander of the Stonington commercial sealing fleet Nathaniel had previously joined, warned him to "have as little communication with the main as possible." This referred to the "Spanish Main," the term American sailors used for Spanish ships sailing in the West Indies to keep control of the South American countries they had ruled for hundreds of years.[1]

Young men from the New England towns had grown up learning how to evade blockading British ships; they had been seasoned by sailing through the violent storms, ice masses, and other dangers in the south polar seas. But they were also trained to figure out how and where they might make money from their voyages. Often, the greater the risk, the greater the reward. When they gradually acquired personal financial interests in the vessels they captained, their willingness to sail where more prudent heads would have stayed home only grew. They observed that bold captains often became the part owners of the ships they sailed.

After returning home, Nathaniel ignored the previous prudent instructions of his former leader, Captain Pendlelton, and deliberately turned to the high-risk waters of the Spanish Main, or West Indies. At the age of twenty-three he had decided to leave the Stonington sealing fleet led by Pendleton and become an individual sea captain for hire by independent ship-owners, many of whom were now sending their vessels to that area.

Captain Palmer's first voyage after leaving the Stonington flotilla fur seal trade was to take his former command, the sloop *John Monroe* to St. Barts in the West Indies in 1822. It had just been purchased by a ship merchant, Henry Trowbridge of New Haven, Connecticut. On this short voyage of only twenty-nine days, his cargo going down was 175 sheep, and he returned with a cargo of sugar.

However, young Captain Palmer made the mistake of undertaking this voyage without a written contract. The ship merchant took advantage of his inexperience, paying him only thirty silver dollars. Trowbridge allegedly explained the modest payment by telling him: "I do not think it is good policy for a young man to have too much money. They are very apt to make a bad use of it."[2]

Captain Palmer had left the relatively safe shipping world led by senior Stonington sea captains where everyone knew and supported each other. This first venture beyond his home port began to teach him the different skills he would need to be a successful captain.

Palmer's swift trip to St. Barts was noticed by others in the shipping world. His next, larger assignment was to take the schooner *Cadet* to Cartagena, Colombia. This vessel was owned by Baldwin & Spooner, a noted shipping company in New York. He made the voyage with American mercantile goods and returned with a cargo for American ports. The voyage was not well documented, but the story has it that the Colombians at first refused to pay full price for the cargo but later relented and covered his demand.[3]

Soon, a totally different set of opportunities in the Caribbean surfaced for Captain Palmer and other intrepid American sea captains. Simon Bolivar, born to an upper-class family in Venezuela, incited a series of revolutions to free the northern South American countries from Spain. He led local armies to liberate Colombia in 1819, Venezuela and Panama in 1821, Ecuador in 1822, Peru in 1824, and Bolivia in 1825.

Bolivar was called "El Libertador." He had climbed with his ragtag forces from the low-lying jungles in Venezuela up over the daunting mountains protecting the border with neighboring Colombia to defeat the forces there commanded by the Spanish who controlled the country. El Libertador continued his success in the adjoining countries of northern South America. He needed resources such as men, arms, ammunition, food stuffs and other supplies required to achieve these hard-fought victories against the Spaniards and to retain control of the countries he had conquered. These supplies and men began to be shipped by Captain Nathaniel Palmer and others in and out of Caribbean ports such as Cartagena, Colombia, throughout the mid and late 1820s.

In terms of the danger to his crew, himself, and his ship, Captain Palmer's shift from sealing in the dangerous waters of the south polar seas to running guns and men for Simon Bolivar only increased the risks he confronted. It was not always certain which faction might control an unruly local Caribbean port when an American ship entered. It was always possible to be plundered or taken over by a Spanish or other privateer. There was often no source of backup an American sailor could rely on from a stable government in these uncertain ports. Officials who controlled these ports could be and often were highly unreasonable.

The Naval Affairs' "volumes of 'American State Papers'" contain many references to the danger American mercantile vessels encountered sailing in the Caribbean at this time:

The extent to which the system of plunder upon the
ocean is carried on in the West India seas and Gulf
of Mexico is truly alarming. … [S]ome fresh instance
of the atrocity with which the pirates carry out
their depredations accompanied by indiscriminate
massacre of the defenseless is brought by every mail
to the House of Representatives.
… This system of piracy is now spreading …
attracting the vicious and desperate of all nations.
March 2, 1822.[4]

Nathaniel wrote a letter in 1824 to his friend, William Fanning,
indicating the risks he and other American mariners faced trading
with South and Central American ports on the Caribbean coasts.
William, like himself, was captaining merchant ships in the West
Indies. The young captains kept their boyhood friends from
Stonington informed of the mutual dangers they would confront
trading there.

March 21, 1824, Port of Cartagena

Dear William,

They claimed we had gone Contrary to the laws
of the country by exporting specie…that we had
infringed on the coasting Laws of the country…
We produced the Law and confronted them…We
produced every requisite paper. …We employed a
lawyer…who drew up necessary papers and presented
them to a judge who has had two weeks promising
every day to send them to a judge to dispatch us, but
it is evident he means to try our patience, as every
one of them from the highest to the lowest are void
of Truth or anything in the shape of it.
They have been accusing me of committing more
sins than I shallever answer if I should live longer

than Moses…I have lost one man with the yellow
fever and have had three sick … but are in a fair way
of Recovery. I cannot tell when I shall be home—at
present the prospect looks dark. Most People in the
United States have a very exalted Opinion of the
Colombians, I only want them to reside in the sinks of
Pollution. Wishing you every Blessing the Heaven can
impart…Excuse the imperfect scroll since I am now
half crazy.

Nathaniel Palmer[5]

Captain Palmer was detained at port for a month and
contracted yellow fever. He lost his hair and when it grew back
it had changed from light brown to a darker color. He was a big
man, but when he regained his health after the yellow fever, he
became an even larger, powerful fellow who commanded respect
wherever he went.

In a brief letter to his mother written a few months later.
Nathaniel didn't discuss the challenges he was facing in the West
Indies. Mercy Brown Palmer must have been constantly worried
about her son's health and safety:

July 4, 1824, New York

Dear Mother,

We depart tomorrow for Cartagena with full freight
on board … including $3700 worth of property
consigned to myself on which I am fortunate to
make good sales.

I subscribe myself your affectionate son.
Nathaniel B. Palmer[6]

Captain Palmer then carried prisoners—Spaniards Bolivar
had captured—on a short voyage from Cartagena to Cuba in

the West Indies. Despite a difficult beginning in Colombia, he obviously had managed to persuade men from a much different culture to entrust him with performing dangerous sailing missions for them. In a follow-up letter to William Fanning, he described his greatly improved relations with the Colombian government. Apparently, Nathaniel had not recently written his mother, since he asked William to communicate with his family:

August 30, 1824, Chagres Panama

Dear William,
After our arrival here in Chagres, Panama 40 hours
out of Cartagena, we discharged our troops and
cargo. I have made a contract with the Colombian
government to transport 70 Divisions from there to
Cuba, with them providing everything necessary for
the voyage. They will clear me from all Port charges
in this country and at Cuba and are to pay me
$9,000 US on Board previous to sailing from Port
the 4th of September… Give my love to the family as
I have not had time to write them.
Yrs, Nathaniel Palmer[7]

William continued in the West Indies to captain the *Bunker Hill* built for him by his father, Edmund Fanning. However, William, unlike Nathaniel, was not able to survive the case of tropical yellow fever he picked up in a Colombian port. Thomas Breed, mate of the *Bunker Hill*, wrote to William's father:

March 11, 1826

Dear Captain Fanning,

It is impossible for me to describe my feelings while
I attempt the painful task of informing you of the
death of your only son, William, who departed

33

this life on the evening of 26 Feb. He had been
complaining of intermittent fever, and his disorder
worsened … in spite of every effort he expired and
was sorrowfully committed to the deep.[8]

Considering the sad final days of other Stonington captains of
the 1820s, Nathaniel and his brother Alex were either unusually
skilled dealing with the variety of difficult challenges facing
American seafarers of that time, unusually lucky, or both.

Later, Alex's sister Juliet Palmer Fanning, warned him of what
had recently happened to two senior Stonington sea captains:

September 1, 1828, New York

Dear Brother,

Brother—Captain Isaac Pendelton's men just stole
his smaller boats. All men left him except two mates
and a boy. He had to sell his brig with all that was
in her for five thousand and some odd dollars and
returned home. Pa says what was in the brig alone
would have sold for two or three thousand dolls…
No doubt he did the best he could. I write you about
it now to put you on your guard with respect to your
men. Another sad story for you-Capt James Sheffield,
Master of the packet ship *Bogota* of New York, put
an end to his life in Gibraltar in May by shooting
himself in the head. What made him commit
the rash act no one can tell. [Sheffield had been
Nathaniel's Master Captain during his voyage to the
South Shetland Islands eight years before]

Affectionate sister, Juliet[9]

Brothers Nathaniel and Alex continued to have their share
of disasters but survived them. Nathaniel's next voyage taking

the *Cadet* back to Cartagena from New York ended when the ship was driven ashore in New Jersey during a severe storm. He and Alexander managed to save the crew, but the ship was a total loss. Often losing a ship would disqualify a captain from future command, but soon after Nathaniel was given command of a larger vessel, the brig *Tampico*. He had established such a reputation as a reliable, successful captain that this disaster did not affect his ability to obtain commands.

Alex joined him as first mate on many of the *Tampico*'s following voyages to the West Indies and Europe from 1826 to 1828, as well as captaining a few himself. During this period, Captain Nathaniel Palmer managed to buy an interest in the *Tampico*. This was an example not only of the ability of a man then still in his twenties to eventually become a ship owner but also demonstrated the fluidity of the market for shares of ships in the early nineteenth century. Investors, ship owners, and captains bought and sold interests in these vessels almost like shares of stocks are traded today. He and the other owners of the *Tampico* sold the ship in 1828 for $5,300, making a fine profit.

Earlier, Edmund Fanning had written Nathaniel's oldest sister, Anne Adelaide, describing her brother Alex's role captaining the *Tampico* in a victory sail over another ship, the *Athenian*. He also reported a trip Nathaniel was currently making. Stonington seafaring families made a continued effort to keep each other well informed.

June 1826, New York

Anne Adelaide,

Alex beat the *Athenian*, Mr Foster [Investor in
the *Tampico]* writes on their passage out, and that
he is highly pleased with him as captain, Alex
is everything he could wish for and so said his
Passengers. The *Tampico* has sail'd for to land some
freight and passengers (for which he got 1200 Doll's)

at Puerto Cabello up the coast which would take
12-20 days & from there direct to New York.
Nathaniel, say to Eliza, sail'd from the currenteen
on Sunday morning last in fine health and in good
spirits. Say to Capt Ben, his Cassandra & Eliza &
all other family friends how, de do for us, and that
we wish you all the best of Heaven's Blessings. Your
little niece Sarah is at my elbow a chatting away but
I cannot for the life of me understand one word she
says, she may be directing me to mention her, to her
Aunt Nancy, or Uncle William, or Uncle Theodore,
for aught I can understand. My wife & Juliet are
well & join with me in our affectionate love to all
our friends.

Your friend, E. Fanning[10]

Edmund Fanning, the family's senior sea captain, had assumed
the role of patriarch, guiding the young captains Nathaniel and
Alex. Later he sent this letter to Alex advising him how to arrange
the best sale of his fur seal skins at Stonington market.

June 23, 1829, New York

Capt Alex Palmer

Your favour of 19inst is received. It was a very
welcome one, I can assure you, Alex my young
friend, and gave to me and Juliet
much pleasure to hear of your arrival in health &
with a good voyage…
Your skins, I am of the opinion, will if in fine order
(which I have no doubt) sell higher than any has
heretofore sold in Stonington. … I shall try to be at
Stonington a day or two before your sale. … Juliet
sends her love & will write she says the next packet,

think Adelaide must have been very pleased in your meeting with [her husband] Capt Charles Stanton.

Your ever sincere friend, Edmund Fanning[11]

The year before Edmund wrote Alex about selling his skins, Juliet had also become knowledgeable enough to give her brother market intelligence. In a passage from her letter quoted above she shares her information with brother Alex:

September 1, 1828

Dear Brother,

Perhaps you think I have forgotten you from my not writing you by the vessels, but be assured my dear brother, that I have not. I often think of you too long in a distant land. Hope you will be successful; and make a good voyage.
Skins are very high. Pa received by the last arrivals from London the sale of a lot that were sold at Baltimore, and shipped there, the owners made a dollar and a half on a skin.

Affectionate sister, Juliet Fanning[12]

Charles Thompson Stanton had married Nathaniel's sister Ann Adelaide in 1827, and six years after Ann's death, he married her younger sister Nancy in 1833. His brother, Joseph Warren Stanton, had married another Palmer sister, Grace in 1821. The Stanton brothers eventually settled in New Orleans. They realized the importance this port would have in world trade and the opportunities it offered.

New Orleans eventually became the fifth largest port in the United States and the most important one dealing with the West Indies and Mexico. Products from the upper American middle west were being shipped down the Mississippi river for export to these markets. Nathaniel's younger brother Louis Lambert had established a trading company with Mexico in New Orleans in 1828. Other Stonington people settled and began to create businesses there.

Here is a letter to Juliet from her brother-in-law Joseph describing a visit to New Orleans with her sister Grace. Note the religious tone of so much of the Palmer family related intimate correspondence:

February 14, 1830, New Orleans

Dear Juliet,

Well, here we are at the famous 'Imporium of the West'. I must say what a strange looking place it is— there is no Eastern city I can compare it to. … Here is an indescribable oddness about the place…. It is not difficult to believe it is destined at no distant period of becoming the first City in the *Union*, perhaps in the world. … This is the mighty Mississippi-The Father of Rivers … Her path too is by the home of the Indian, when he walks as lord & proprietor of the forest, where he exists in his pride & nobleness.

We saw the store of Palmer & Co soon after we landed and thought how different we should feel if our dear Lambert was still its occupier. [Nathaniel and Juliet's brother, Lambert Palmer, had died prematurely of fever at 25 in 1829 while in Vera Cruz, Mexico, having begun trading from his New Orleans office the year before.] Others too are gone…

Let us mourn them, by living as they all would have wished us to.

… When this brief human travel has ended, when the

38

shadows of Death are closing about our Eyes, let us be prepared for the Change and resign in confidence and peace, the spirit which God has given us.

Yrs truly, Joseph Warren Stanton[13]

Two of Charles and Joseph Stanton's younger brothers, Alexander and Horatio Stanton, had also gone to New Orleans to make their fortunes but unfortunately died there from the local tropical diseases in 1839 and 1842. Nathaniel's wife, Eliza, had a brother, Giles Babcock, who with a partner created the trading firm there of Phelps & Babcock. New Orleans became an enticing place for people from Stonington to visit relatives and friends.

In 1836, Nathaniel and Eliza Palmer went to New Orleans as the guests of Jedediah Leeds, whose family had built a substantial business there. In 1838, Juliet Palmer Fanning traveled to New Orleans on brother Alex's ship the *Louisville*, where she joined sister-in-law Priscilla.

Juliet gave her first impression of the view of New Orleans' famous levee at the mouth of the Mississippi:

> Have at last the sight of New Orleans, from a sudden
> bend of the river, it looks quite imposing. ... The
> Exchange on Charles Street, shows nobly, its Dome
> towering above everything around it. The
> city lays like a crescent on the river, forming an
> amphitheater which cannot be comprehended at
> first. ...We ran directly along the side of the levee,
> where the vessels lay one after the other to a long
> distance, and the steamboats (which had come down
> the Mississippi) look like floating palaces with their
> cabins on deck, one and two stories high. ... We
> followed the course of the levee for
> sometime through the great quantities of molasses
> and sugar barrels, huge piles of cotton bales, men

speaking almost all of the languages on earth.
Women with tables covered with eatables of all sorts,
from the bacon of Ohio to the fruits of the Tropics.[14]

Summers in New Orleans could be dangerous because of its epidemics of tropical diseases, malaria, cholera, and yellow fever. They took people like Alexander and Horatio Stanton away in the prime of life. The medical world had not yet discovered sure cures for these illnesses. Stonington area people who visited over the years often planned their visits to avoid the summers. Joseph Warren Stanton and William Lord Palmer, one of Nat's younger brothers who also became a sea captain, went on to live in New Orleans until the 1870s.[15]

Captain Nathaniel Palmer then received another opportunity to establish his growing reputation as a mariner. Mr. J.N. Reynolds believed the United States government should finance needed exploration of both the South Seas and north Pacific, not only to gain scientific understanding of these regions, but also to establish American rights to territories discovered. Reynolds spent months trying to persuade the United States Congress and President Jackson to provide U.S. government financing for an expedition like Captain Bellinghausen's discovery voyage for the Russian Government a decade earlier. After much political skirmishing, President Jackson's administration turned the request down.[16]

Reynolds did not give up. He appealed to the sentiments of the ship owners of Stonington, who considered the rebuke from Washington D.C. an affront to their pride and to their previous efforts of discovery such as Antarctica. Edmund Fanning, Benjamin Pendleton, and Nathaniel Palmer agreed to participate in the voyage, with Fanning taking on most of its expense.

Its flagship was the brig *Annawan*, then owned by Benjamin Pendleton, Commodore of the Stonington sealing fleet expedition of 1820–1822. Nathaniel Palmer captained it; J.N. Reynolds and several scientists were aboard this specially equipped vessel that sailed out in October 1829 determined to collect flora and fauna, link with native people in the regions explored, and discover territories for the United States.

Another ship in the group from Stonington was the schooner *Penguin* captained by younger brother Alexander Palmer. The brig *Seraph* made up the third ship. It was understood the three vessels would also engage in sealing in the south seas to help finance the expedition. Whatever seal skins or seal oil they obtained would be sent back to Stonington by another ship before they sailed to the North Pacific. It turned out to be a very long voyage beyond their expectations.

The extremely difficult weather the ships encountered going round Cape Horn and up the southern Pacific coast of South America made it hard to keep them together. Seals were scarce, and no new discoveries of territories were made. The captains also had trouble with their crews who became concerned with the mediocre sealing returns obtained, since their pay depended on successful sealing harvests. The captains and sponsors of the expedition had been willing to sacrifice profits for the scientific-discovery objectives of the trip.[17]

However, these lofty objectives were less important to the ordinary sailors who began to complain. Some of them had to be delivered to the United States Counsel in Valparaiso, Chile by Captain Nathaniel Palmer. Others deserted later during the voyages. Reynolds and a scientist asked to be left with Indians on the Pacific coast so they could establish good relations for future visits by similar expeditions.

Their effort was deemed worthwhile by the Stonington sea captains involved, since it established that American sailors from Stonington were willing to make sacrifices to enhance the future prospects of the United States merchant fleet in international waters.[18]

CHAPTER 5

NATHANIEL *and* ALEX'S WIVES—CAPTAIN PALMER OUTWITS *the* CHILEAN CONVICTS

NATHANIEL BROWN PALMER married Eliza Babcock on December 7, 1826, in Stonington. Eliza was then sixteen years of age and her husband twenty-seven. That difference of eleven years may have been commonplace in the early nineteenth century, but given his experience at sea, Nathaniel's twenty-seven years were equivalent to the life experience few men in our time would be fortunate enough to have by the time they were fifty. Despite her youth, Eliza began to demonstrate the confidence and maturity required to maintain her own position in the marriage.

If the boys of that time in Stonington were expected to act like men, then girls in their mid-teens could act like women. Just before he was about to sail for the West Indies, Nathaniel had written his mother a letter mentioning Eliza. This was almost two years before he married her.

February 25, 1825, Sandy Hook

My dear Mother,

With great pleasure I write you a few lines to advise you of my sailing this day with full freight and a few passengers. I received a letter from the young lady

downtown [Eliza] which I can assure you afforded
me great pleasure. Tell sister Ann she must visit Eliza
often.… The Brig *Abigail* arrived yesterday from
Cartagena at which time the *Bunker Hill* had been
18 days out. …
Hoping that you may soon be returned to health and
that I must see you again.

Your affectionate son, Nathaniel Palmer[1]

At the tender age of fifteen, Eliza was courting the man she had probably decided would be her future husband with her letters to him at sea.

Nathaniel and Alex were fortunate not only as ship captains but also as husbands. Each brother married a spirited young woman who loved and respected him, shared his courage and character, supported him loyally through thick and thin, and waited patiently, often deeply lonely, for him to return from long voyages. This yearning for a sea captain husband's return from a long voyage was the reason widow's walks and cupolas were built on the top of sea captain's houses enabling their wives to earnestly look out for a returning ship bringing their husbands home.

It may be hard for us to imagine today, when a wife now can communicate daily with her husband by email, text, or mobile phone even when he is serving at a battle front in Gaza, Iraq or Ukraine, how wives of sea captains in the nineteenth century must have felt when they were not only separated from their husbands, but also had difficulty communicating with them by letter for up to two or even three years.

To understand why Eliza insisted on accompanying her husband on his next long voyage to the Pacific in 1831, one only has to read her heart-breaking letter to him written the year before when Nathaniel had not yet returned from his lengthy exploration voyage to the Pacific captaining the brig *Annawan:*

April 1, 1830, Stonington

My Dear Husband,

I have been patient, but news came two months ago of Alex's arrival [Alex's ship the *Penguin* had returned much earlier from the same voyage as Nathaniel's], so I thought it was time to hear from you. …Your letters are so precious to me, and I only wish they could be more frequent. …I hope in twelve months more I shall see my husband and not be separated from him again. A good many have told me you would be gone three years, Juliet said so, but I cannot [bear it], it is too long. *When you go again, I will go with you.* [emphasis added].

… I cannot imagine where you now are, perhaps on some cold and dreary island catching seals … or sailing pleasantly along, borne on every wave further from those you love …

Dear Husband, take good care of your health, do come to Stonington with the Brig when you return. Many Blessings attend you wherever you go, is the solemn prayer of your truly affectionate wife, Eliza Palmer[2]

Nathaniel Palmer had many admirable traits, but making the effort to regularly write his young wife left at home does not seem to have been one of them. He appears to have been so carried away by the responsibilities of being a ship captain that he didn't adopt a focused, regular practice of trying to get letters back to Eliza, who was eager for information of what was happening to her husband at sea. His earlier letters from the polar seas and the West Indies to his mother, Mercy before she died in 1826 were also brief, few, and far between.

In the fall of 1831 Captain Palmer took the brig *Annawan* on his second trip from Stonington to the southern Pacific Ocean.

He sailed with a crew of eleven to the Juan Fernandez Islands in the Pacific Ocean 500 miles west of Santiago, Chile. His objective was to buy fur seal skins and other goods the inhabitants sold to mariners. He also assumed he would obtain needed fresh provisions for his crew. The archipelago had been the inspiration for the story of Robinson Crusoe.

As she promised in her letter, Eliza shipped out with her husband. She must have learned from other Stonington women who had accompanied their husbands at sea that she would experience hardships as the only woman aboard. After her recent suffering when she did not see him for years at sea, Eliza decided she wanted to be with her husband. This would be her first of many long voyages with him.

Eliza must have had a fascinating trip with Nathaniel, supported by his welcoming crew, during their two-month voyage from Stonington down 10,000 miles of the Atlantic Ocean. When they finally reached Cape Horn at the bottom of South America, Captain Nathaniel Palmer still had to sail through the notoriously dangerous waters south of it separating the Atlantic and Pacific oceans. The couple then had a meaningful further journey north into the Pacific to reach their destination. Accustomed as Eliza must have been to hearing of the dangers of the sea from Stonington mariner families and friends, she never could have anticipated the dangers awaiting them in Robinson Crusoe's islands.

The Juan Fernandez archipelago far out in the Pacific Ocean from Chile included a large island that the Chilean Government used as a major penal colony. Chile and other Spanish-controlled countries often permitted the wives of prisoners to live with them while serving their sentences. On December 31, 1831, the *Annawan* arrived and dropped anchor just off this main island. Nathaniel remarked to Eliza that it was strange that the beach was deserted; usually everyone came to greet any large ship arriving at an island. Early the next morning he took a few men in his long boat and rowed into the beach to see if anything was wrong.[3]

Shortly thereafter, a Chilean brig came within hailing distance of the *Annawan* to warn that the convicts had overtaken their jailors on the island. They were preparing to board Captain Palmer's ship, take her over, and use her as their escape ship. Since he had just left his ship to go to shore, he was completely unaware of the extreme conditions he would encounter.

When the convicts first saw the *Annawan* approaching their island, they were worried she might sail to Valparaiso, the nearest city on the Chilean coast, to warn authorities of their revolt. But later when they saw Captain Palmer approaching their island in a small boat, they realized they could capture him and then use his vessel to take them to safety. A group of armed convicts waited for his small party in the underbrush just off the beach where he landed. They seized Nathaniel and his sailors, blindfolded them, and took them to the prison chapel to meet the leaders of their rebellion.

When their blindfolds were removed, Nathaniel and his men faced a mob of 100 outlaws from various South American countries. They had fled to Chile's coast to escape prosecution elsewhere. In Chile they continued to pirate innocent vessels and perform other forms of robbery. This dangerous group of criminals had been captured by Chilean authorities and sent to their island penal colony.

One of them proposed they kill Captain Palmer so it would be easy to take over his ship for their escape. The mob shouted their approval. He was blindfolded again and taken to a wall of the church to be shot by mutineers armed with muskets. However, during the previous threatening mob discussion, Nathaniel, who had learned Spanish, began chanting a secret password to indicate that he was a member of the ancient, honorable fraternity of Freemasons.

The Freemasons were the oldest fraternal organization in the world. They were founded in thirteenth-century Europe and gradually grew over the centuries to have lodges in almost every Western nation. They were a secret group whose members had faith in a religion, and pledged to improve the world and protect each other when in danger. They operated with a series of secret handshakes and oaths known only to themselves, empowering a member to declare his status to fellow Masons wherever he might be. Simon Bolivar had been an active Freemason when Nathaniel was working for his cause in the West Indies during the mid-1820s.

Fortunately, the convict leader who had planned the uprising was a fellow Mason. He heard Nathaniel's chant and proceeded to protect him. Winking at him, he stepped forward, explaining to his compatriots it would be better for them to spare the *Annawan*'s captain, so they could use him as a helpful hostage. He then loudly told him in front of the mob that he had two choices: 1) Either be shot now, or 2) Promise to take the rebels safely to the mainland at a place of their choosing without informing the Chilean authorities. Nathaniel agreed with the latter, understanding his fellow Mason had saved his life.[4]

Captain Palmer then sent a note written in English to his first mate by one of his captured sailors, ordering him to prepare to receive the convicts. He also managed to hide in the note another message to his mate on board the *Annawan*. This ordered him to clear out a spare storeroom on the ship where bread had been stored and to put Mrs. Palmer in it while advising her to make no noise or activity that would betray her to the convicts. No part of the room should emit much light or sound.

Another challenge Nathaniel faced was the desire of the convicts' women to be taken on board the *Annawan*. If this occurred, at least two serious risks would be created: 1) In the close quarters of the vessel it was likely that the convicts could resort to fighting over the women among themselves, destabilizing the ship; 2) Even more important, the convicts' women would be taken into the *Annawan*'s cabin, where they would eventually discover that Eliza was hidden on the ship. Nathaniel had received a promise from his fellow Mason that only the male convicts would be taken on board.

In the excitement of the boarding, some of the convicts' women managed to climb into the small boats taking their men to the ship. Upon arriving at the *Annawan*, they boarded her with great noise and animation. By this time, Captain Palmer was released and had immediately returned to his ship. This was not the slim lad in seal skins who had met with Captain Bellinghausen off the great continent of Antarctica a decade ago. This was the over six-foot commanding sea captain with dark brown hair and beard who had overcome so many daunting challenges in his previous decade at sea. With confidence, he walked the deck of his ship firmly ordering the convicts to take their women back to the island. Instinctively, the men obeyed his instructions.[5]

During the time before they could reach Chile, the 100 dangerous brigands roamed the ship. There was an upheaval when some feared they would be delivered to a Chilean Man of War, but their convict leader continued to convince them Captain Palmer would get them to the mainland. Eliza was restricted to her small storeroom and somehow the crew was able to provide her with water and food. The only way Nathaniel could reassure her was to issue loud orders to his crew while walking as close to her hiding place as possible. She bravely spent her ten days of total isolation in fearsome conditions without complaint. The wind was light, and it would be ten days before the brig reached the shore of Chile.[6]

When land was finally sighted, Captain Palmer fulfilled his promise by sending all the convicts to shore in his small boats. They scattered inland, where eventually they began bothering local Chileans. Eventually they were captured again by the Chilean authorities and put on a ship in Valparaiso Harbor to be returned to their penal colony with its waiting women. Local lore has it that when their Chilean brig passed close by the *Annawan*, also in harbor, the convicts shouted their appreciation: "Los buenos, Americanos!"[7]

Despite the unexpected experience with the convicts, Nathaniel was able to buy seal skins and other products, which he shipped home by another vessel. He continued his trading efforts along the coasts of Chile and Peru on the *Annawan* with Eliza at his side for more than another year. She had managed to have the sailing experience of a lifetime while shipping out as the only woman on board. The couple finally left the Chilean coast for home on July 9, 1833. They arrived in Stonington at 10 a.m., September 25, 1833. Eliza's first cruise with her husband had lasted a full two years.

Eliza was not without male admirers. She and Nathaniel had become friends with Captain Francis H. Gregory, an American naval officer who eventually became a rear admiral. Gregory came from a well-connected New England background. He kept up a correspondence with Eliza and Nathaniel for years, offering to introduce them to prominent families he knew in important sailing ports throughout the world, all while singing Eliza's praises. When not at sea, Gregory lived with his wife and children in a large house in New Haven, Connecticut, called The Anchorage. Here is an example of his attentions to Eliza:

November 6, 1837, The Anchorage,
New Haven, Connecticut

Dear Eliza,

Oh you runaway. What shall I call you-or how shall
I punish you for disappointing all the hopes and
expectations of your friends at the Anchorage. I will
disappoint you in turn—by forgiving you—and
once more address you as I have been wont to, as
being still that dear Sister whose remembrance has
been so constantly and affectionately cherished, and
whose presence never fails to diffuse so much joy
and happiness.
…But you must allow me to scold a little upon this
occasion as my disappointment is severely felt. …As
I may say it has even been doubled upon me having
been deprived of the pleasure of meeting you last
summer. …It is not long since you honored me with
the affectionate appellation of Brother. May I still my
Dear sister, look for the enjoyment in your society
which that relationship warrants for the affectionate

confidence of a sister.
Now my dear sister, comes the scolding I set out in a
finale from Tom Moore—
"They know not my heart, who believe there can be ..."

I am yr affectionate friend, F. H. Gregory[8]

Gregory's continued interest in Eliza was illustrated six months
later in a letter Eliza wrote Nathaniel as he was sailing from New
York that also illustrates how his voyages affected her:

March 7, 1838, Astor House, New York

My dear Husband,

I watched you from the top of the Astor House
cupola until the tall masts were hidden from my
sight ... and I could not restrain my tears.
... I could scarcely realize you were gone, so
confident was I of seeing you again. Capt. Gregory
was with me and finally entered into my feelings.
... When the gentlemen came into dinner they
were surprised that you were gone, but I told them
I had seen you through the narrows. ... Saturday,
Capt. Gregory took Mama and me to the Zoological
Institute. We met Capt. Roger there, who was quite
sociable with Capt. Gregory. He was very much
surprised to find who I was, thought me more Capt.
G's daughter.

With much love, I remain your fond wife Eliza.[9]

Eliza's sister-in- law, Priscilla Dixon, six years younger than she,
married Nathaniel's younger brother Alexander in June 1837. Eliza
described their pending marriage in a letter to Juliet Fanning. She
and Nathaniel had now been married for eleven years:

May 29, 1837

Dear Sister,

Do you know when A & P are to be married? I have
not had the opportunity of asking her since Alex
just returned from a voyage. They appear very happy
together, she is a lovely girl and I feel that Alex will
have as good a wife as he deserves …

Your affectionate sister, Eliza[10]

In November of 1837, five months after their wedding, Priscilla
wrote to Alex, who had just left on a voyage of nine weeks and
had been away for two.

November 12, 1837

My dear husband,

How are you now? O if I could see you a little
while—my dear husband. When I think that only
2 weeks of 9 long weeks are past, I cannot but feel
very, very sad. … You have no idea how much
comfort your miniature affords me. Eliza sits beside
me writing and sends much love to you. … *I think I
shall not be willing you should leave me again*-not that
I am sorry that I did not accompany you as really I
have never been sorry, because you thought it best
for me to stay and that is quite comforting, after all,
I did that which it was my duty to do-but I shall not
be *unwilling to accompany you in January* [Alex's next
voyage], *will you be sorry to have me?*

Your own Priscilla[11]

What young husband could resist such a letter from his adoring wife? She soon began accompanying Alex on voyages. Priscilla wrote in her diary on Christmas day 1838: "This day left home with my husband for New York…the beginning of our journey together to New Orleans on the good ship *Louisville*. On Saturday 20th of January we landed safely in New Orleans having executed but one storm. …O how thankful should we be to the Great Being who has thus preserved us through dangers seen and unseen."[12]

Priscilla accompanied Alex on several of his subsequent voyages despite the four children she bore him from 1840 through 1848. Eliza, their grandparents, other family members, and housekeepers in Stonington were always there to take care of them.

Ten years later, Priscilla was still very much in love with her husband. She wrote to Alex in a message demonstrating the Palmers' willingness to help people in need. The potato famine was just beginning to ravage Ireland:

May 20, 1847, Westerly, RI

My dear Husband,

We reached home safely this morning. The children seem very good & have been happy all day. Natty [their oldest child] has attended school and is much pleased to get back. I never felt so sad and lonely as I did yesterday just before we left New York. I heard nothing from you in the mail and all was dark and dismal. Mary, Harriet's Irish girl, is in great trouble-she got a letter saying her family are in great distress & want to come here to us. Will you not be kind enough to write them and tell them when to come and that you will take them. Direct it to the care of Pat Conaghan, Edgeworthstown, County Westmeath, Ireland.
May you be watched over & protected & soon

restored to your own fond wife—is my most earnest
prayer. I wish myself with you very often. This
will be sent by the 'Queen of the West' as she sails
tomorrow. I shall write at every opportunity. Mother
sends a great deal of love. Your own, Priscilla.[13]

Nathaniel and Alex's families had become so closely knit that
any commitment, like the one made to the Irish girl, Mary, would
have been accepted by the other.

Despite the difference in their ages and times of their marriages,
Eliza and Priscilla became close friends. They provided desperately
needed mutual support for each other when their husbands were
away. There were no telephones, undersea cables, or other devices
to keep them connected with their men who went to sea for
years at a time. They had to depend on the delivery of personal
mail other ship Captains handed over to friends on passing ships
thousands of miles away in Europe, South America, or Asia. The
fraternity of mariners made a special effort to help each other
keep in touch with their families left on shore.

An excerpt from Priscilla's diary of January 1838 indicates the
limits women like herself and her sister-in-law Eliza were expected
to live within:

"On Sunday morning I went to hear a sermon from
Mr. Clapp on the station, position and characteristics
of women. He allowed us to be equal to, not inferior
to the males, but we should exert our influence at
home in the domestic circle, and women should be
religious. He said Religion was made for women."[14]

These supposed boundaries did not appear to limit either lady
in confronting their powerful sea captain husbands. Many years
later in 1851, Eliza rebuked her husband who had neglected to
write her. Apparently Nathaniel was not at sea, Eliza had simply
gone down the Connecticut coast from Stonington to stay with
friends in Saybrook for a few weeks:

July 14, 1851 Saybrook, Connecticut

My dear husband,

I am much surprised and disappointed at not
hearing from you since I left Stonington. I think
it is really unkind not to write to me a line and I
cannot account for it…I hoped you wanted to see
me enough to come or at least to write and ask me
when I was coming home. There has been such a fine
breeze today that I have been looking for you-yet I
am not ready to go-but I do want to hear from you.
Your aff wife Eliza.[15]

There have been several studies of women like Eliza and
Priscilla who went to sea with their captain husbands in the
nineteenth century. Interestingly, the few ladies who shipped out
as captains' wives all agreed on what they most missed during
these long voyages. This was the opportunity to converse with
other women.[16]

CAPTAIN PALMER INSPIRES *the* BLUE-WATER AMERICAN FLEET *to* COMPETE *with* ENGLAND

THE TWENTY-YEAR-OLD CAPTAIN Nathaniel Brown Palmer who sailed his forty-seven-foot sloop *Hero* ten thousand miles down the Atlantic to eventually "discover" Antarctica in 1820 developed into an experienced captain who took his crews on larger vessels up and down the Atlantic and Pacific Coasts, to the south polar seas, and throughout the Caribbean. But his subsequent role in the American maritime history of the middle nineteenth century transcends these experiences. In this second stage of his maritime career Captain Nathaniel Palmer became the American sea captain from Stonington who gradually showed his colleagues how to challenge England's dominance as the leading maritime blue-water international trader.

At the beginning of the nineteenth century, the growing US maritime fleet was far behind England in its ability to trade with the world over its great oceans-the Atlantic and Pacific. By the mid-1850s when Nathaniel finally retired as an active sea captain, they were full-fledged challengers of England's mastery of blue-water sailing around the world.

The terms "blue-water" and "brown-water" sailing are described as follows. Brown-water sailing is sailing from port to port along the North or South American coasts or nearby waters like the Caribbean where the ocean has a brownish color by virtue of the shallow coastal waters being colored by the brown earth, mud, and sand. When the sail was from one coast like southern Florida to a nearby coast like Cuba, the term brown-water may be applied. It also applied to shipping up and down great internal rivers like the Mississippi, or even to shipping on the great lakes where the land was never that far away.

Blue-water sailing is used to describe trips going across the great oceans like the Atlantic or Pacific. Vessels going from New York or Boston to London or Liverpool across the Atlantic, or to India or China via the Cape of Good Hope in southern Africa, or from those American cities around the Horn in southern South America and then up and across the vast Pacific Ocean to Canton, China, would be blue-water journeys.

By the time Nathaniel returned with Eliza from his voyage up the Pacific coast of South America on September 25, 1833, he had established himself as a successful captain who could deliver for ship owners no matter what challenges might be encountered. Beginning in the late 1820s Captain Palmer was already beginning to become personally wealthy from the profits of his voyages and investment in the ships he captained. In the early 1830s he could have settled down to enjoy life as a highly successful skipper and ship owner in the American brown-water trade.[1]

Most American shipping during the years before Nathaniel was born up until the early 1830s when he returned to Stonington with Eliza was dominated by brown-water voyages up and down the Atlantic Coast and into the Caribbean, rather than long voyages across the oceans to England or China. Early American merchant mariners and sea captains as well as those after the Revolutionary War concentrated on carrying the significant trade which existed between Americans themselves and with their neighbors. Fish, livestock, grain, rum, and finished cotton goods were traded by the northern merchants and mariners for the sugar, flour, molasses, tobacco and cotton from southern states they brought back. American ships also carried some of these products plus finished English goods back to the north Atlantic coast from islands in the Caribbean. Merchant mariners all along the entire Atlantic coast constantly traded:

salted fish, pork, other foodstuffs, timber, and a range of other basic products with each other.[2]

During the first fifty years of Nathaniel Palmer's life the United States had significant population growth. The New England states had the best with their higher birth rate 3 percent and lower death rate 1 percent due to their cold winters which killed disease-bearing insects bearing the tropical diseases prevalent in the southern states. From 1800 to 1850 America's population increased from 5 million people to 23 million. Here are the increases from decade to decade: 1800–5.3M; 1810–7.2M; 1820–9.6M; 1830–12.9M; 1840–17M; 1850–23.1M. This population increase, coupled with Nathaniel's dynamic role in the shipping industry driving New England's economic growth, gave him the base to accomplish what he did.[3]

Fortunes were made by the American merchants who owned the vessels and their sea captains who received shares in the ships they captained as did Nathaniel Palmer. Fortunes were also lost when the ships of these adventurous Americans were seized by English privateers, French privateers off the Atlantic coast, or even by Barbary pirates when the American merchants were bold enough to venture into their territory.[4] No one understood the high risks and equally high profits which could be experienced in this shipping market better than Captain Palmer.

But something in his nature led Nathaniel Palmer to venture beyond the brown-water coastal markets where he could have completed a highly rewarding career. Eleven years before at age twenty-three he had demonstrated his adventurous spirit by leaving the Stonington sealing fleet to become an independent sea captain. He was also fortunate enough to have Edmund Fanning, part of his extended family, as one of his key mentors. By sailing around the world in the 1790s, Captain Fanning had already demonstrated that a son of Stonington could master blue-water sailing.

Captain Nathaniel Palmer also believed sailing had a higher calling than mere profits. In October 1829 he had captained the *Annawan* around the Horn and up the Chilean coast on an earlier scientific-exploration expedition to polar seas and the Pacific Ocean. The voyage had been primarily financed by Edmund Fanning.[5]

Like his mentor Fanning, Captain Palmer was fascinated by what new challenges he could overcome; he was never content to rest on his laurels. He became obsessed by the concept of what an ideal sea captain should be. Nathaniel finally figured out what qualities this captain should have and adopted them for himself. He would be the captain who: a) Always made the fastest passages from point to point, and b) Always arrived on time regardless of i) Terrible weather with turbulent seas, and/or ii) A challenging crew.

By the mid-1830s Captain Palmer became known as a skipper who stayed up all night on deck, leading his crews to bring in their ships to make record times from port to port. He drove his men to make their schedules, no matter how bad the stormy weather, or even lack of wind. He strove to always be dependable. Here is an example of his behavior:

"While the ship plunged and plowed her way to eastward the captain remained on deck, no matter how competent the junior officers, for he alone was responsible for the speed of the passage and the safety of the ship. All night he paced the quarterdeck… The captain sat down for a rest… ,but never did he fail to give heed to the wet sails and the straining gear aloft. His meals were brought to him…but he was on his feet, pacing to and fro or walking forward for a look at the head sails during many more hours of the day than he was seated…The next night found him as vigilant as ever. For him there was no watch below. Day on day and night on night he turned his eyes from the reeling spars to the raging seas and back again to the spars…He was chilled by the wind as well as the water; but he remained on deck, ready on the instant for every emergency, while the storm lasted."[6]

These traits of speed and dependability brought him to the attention of two parties who would have a determining effect on his future career as a sea captain and ship designer from 1833 to 1855. They were Edward Knight Collins, master of the American packet ship fleet, and the Low brothers, merchants and builders of the subsequent American clipper ship fleet.

Working with them Captain Nathaniel Palmer would demonstrate how Americans could design, build and sail superior packet ships to London and Liverpool, and design, build and sail the first American clippers to Canton, China. He would become instrumental in showing American sailors how to successfully challenge the previously dominant English masters of international blue-water trading fleets.

CHAPTER 7

COMMODORE *of* AMERICA'S PACKET
SHIPS *to* ENGLAND

By the time Captain Nathaniel Brown Palmer brought the *Annawan* and his young wife, Eliza, back to Stonington in 1833, he had left his earlier commitment to fur sealing behind. By this time the poor creatures had almost been decimated in the southern Atlantic Ocean by avid sealers from many nations. Simon Bolivar had died and was no longer a potential client. Nathaniel had new worlds to conquer.

His first challenge was to improve the American packet ship fleet. The British had created these packet ships to provide a regular service for passengers and mail traveling from London and Liverpool to and from their far-flung colonies. They derived their name from the packets of mail they carried.

The packet ships enabled British subjects living and serving in the colonies to travel back and forth from their assignments to native England. Those already overseas could keep in touch with their families and friends by mail. Stable communication was provided for the governmental structure that ruled the colonies. The packet ships also could carry cargos like cotton from the American south to Liverpool.

The packets were quite different from the later clipper ships who only carried a few distinguished passengers, and whose main purpose was to carry special bulk cargos such as tea from China to America and Europe, and products desired by China

60

back to it such as ginseng and special woods.

Unlike England, the early United States had no regular service of ships leaving and returning to ports at scheduled times designed for passengers and mail. But in 1817, New York traders founded a line of packet ships, *The Black Ball Line*, which operated regularly between New York and Liverpool, England. They sailed at a regular time each month. There were no delays for weather or other reasons. The first packet ship sailed from New York on January 5, 1818, despite snow falling at the port. Packet lines soon began to regularly sail from major American ports to various destinations in Europe, as well as up and down the east coast of America.[1]

The ideal captain of a packet ship was a man who could make schedules regardless of obstacles such as the gales, high waves, icy conditions, and every type of challenging weather Captain Palmer had already experienced around the south pole. He knew how to adjust the riggings and sails to meet different wind conditions. He also had learned to manage crews that had difficulty or resisted working in such risky conditions, men who might even mutiny if pushed too hard. He was ideally suited for his new role.[2]

Edward Knight (E.K.) Collins, who owned ships carrying goods between New York and New Orleans, asked Nathaniel when he returned to Stonington in 1833 to be one of his key captains taking cotton from the south to New York and eventually across the Atlantic to Liverpool. Captain Palmer accepted his offer and took over Collin's ship the *Huntsville*, a large packet. In the next decade the *Huntsville* would provide Nathaniel with an idea for the first American clipper the *Houqua*, which he helped design ten years later. This was because the *Huntsville's* bottom had deliberately been rounded into a shallow U-shape, enabling it to sail over the sand bar outside New Orleans harbor. Most seamen then believed the classic V-shaped bottom was the best design to get speed out of a ship.[3]

By the time Collins became a leader in the American cotton trade in 1835, he had five ships that sailed monthly in season up and down America's Atlantic coast and then across the Atlantic to Liverpool, England. Several were large packets: the *Huntsville* was 523 tons, and the *Yazoo* was 678 tons. The usual voyage of the *Huntsville* from New Orleans to New York had been eighteen days; Captain Palmer took her there in fourteen days. He also charmed the Southern cotton plantation owners who were Collins's customers with his fine Yankee manners and commanding presence. Captain Palmer then suggested Collins also hire his younger brother Alex as one of his captains, and he did.

In early 1835, Captain Palmer took one of Collins's packets across the Atlantic to Liverpool, and when he arrived studied how the English packets operated. When he returned, he advised Collins that he could effectively compete in the America to England packet trade. Their cargo going over would mainly be cotton, but the ships would also provide a more luxurious berth for American passengers wishing to visit England and Europe. In addition, he suggested that Collins build larger ships than the current packets, which averaged 450 to 600 tons.[4]

Captain Palmer boldly proposed building ships of up to 900 tons or more. Their passenger trade would be enhanced by decorating the cabins with luxurious furnishings—rich rugs, draperies, fine woods, and fancy dining rooms. Finally, the ships would be designed with rounded bottoms and would make faster voyages than their current competitors. Passengers would pay much more for their passage on these vessels than they paid before for any transatlantic crossings. The crewmen on these ships would also be compensated better than those on other vessels and would not have to pay for their food. These jobs became the prime opportunities for the more experienced sailors, who would enhance the performance of their ships.[5]

Collins followed Nathaniel's advice. He had five ships constructed in the Brown & Bell shipyards in New York City. They were called the *Dramatic Line* and were named for the famous actors and authors of leading plays in the theater world. Many in the shipping business felt Collins and Palmer had overreached themselves, but they were soon proved wrong. In 1836, Collins built the *Shakespeare*, the largest packet ship yet constructed. When Captain Palmer took her to Liverpool on her maiden voyage, thousands crowded the docks to witness her arrival. He was becoming known to British leaders in the merchant shipping world.

By then Captain Palmer had agreed with Collins that he would command Collins's new *Dramatic Line* transatlantic fleet of packet ships. They had also agreed that he would be responsible for inspiring the design for nautical architects, and the construction by the leading boat builders Brown & Bell in New York of the twin ships *Garrick* and *Sheridan*, which weighed in at 927 tons. At first, the Brown & Bell yards scoffed at Nathaniel's idea to build the larger packets with flat bottoms. They said it was ridiculous because there was no need for these deep water ships to sail over shallow harbor limitations like the earlier Collins' packets did when picking up cotton on the Mississippi River.

However, when they asked the future great clipper ship designer Donald McKay to comment, McKay supported Nathaniel's design. He opined that his flat-bottomed packets would have more stability in turbulent North Atlantic waters than the current sharp-bottomed vessels designed for ocean travel. The *Garrick* and *Sheridan* proved Palmer and McKay were right. They led to the construction by Collins of the 1,000-ton *Roscius*, the largest, most handsome packet ship of them all.[6]

Captain Palmer was compensated very well. His salary of $30 per month was modest, but he also received 25 percent of passenger revenue and all the fees paid for delivering mail. He was now receiving over $20,000 a year, a handsome sum for that time.

It was clear to the British that the American packet ships had become superior to their British counterparts, although England had originally created this class of vessel to serve its empire. A Committee of Parliament was set up to determine how this had occurred. It concluded: "American ships had a preference over English vessels solely because vessel and crew taken together were more efficient." Much of this praise had been earned by Captain Palmer. He had also become known to the investors and underwriters of his captained vessels as a man who never cost them an extra cent.[7]

During the 1830s, when both Nathaniel and brother Alex captained many packet ships for E.K. Collins, their compensation package was complex. Disputes arose between Alex and E.K. Collins concerning Alex's compensation. This led to a nasty confrontation, but Alex firmly held his ground, resolving their differences. Alex's sister Juliet wrote a letter to her daughter Sarah describing the dispute:

December 6, 1841, New York

Dear Sarah,

I shall buy you some molasses candy while I am out.
… Your Uncle Alex is going to sue Mr. Collins today.
He went to his office. He [Collins] has trumped up
a long one against him about things when he was
in the *Garrick*. … I feel sometimes as if I wanted to
cowhide them myself almost and then I soften down.
Am willing to leave them in the hands of their Great
Judge … [At the end of the long letter, which must
have been written over several days, Juliet closes
with:] Uncle Alex has got his accounts from Collins
without suing him.

Addio ma chere, Juliet[8]

Nathaniel had turned forty-one in 1840, an early age for our time but a more advanced one for a man who had been sailing ships through highly challenging seas since the age of fourteen. In October 1840, he drove the Packet *Siddons* from Liverpool across the Atlantic in fifteen days to her pier in New York. This was the fastest westward passage between those ports on record. The constant strain of being a sea captain who experienced continual extreme demands on his body and mind adversely affected his health and completely exhausted him.

He had helped Collins create an American packet fleet that now rivaled and exceeded the British blue-water packet ships in quality and speed. Even the British shipowners and sea captains acknowledged this. His work with E.K. Collins was completed.

Nathaniel Palmer sailed to Havana, Cuba, as a passenger to enjoy the winter weather there, beginning a year where he relaxed and recovered his health and spirit. He captained only two voyages during this period, both to Brazil. It was recorded that on July 4, 1841, he went fishing off Block Island and caught eighty mackerel.[9]

Captain Nathaniel Brown Palmer would master a new challenge in the final stage of his career as master mariner. He would be the American sea captain whose inspired leadership coordinating the efforts of other nautical experts would produce the first American clipper ship of its time—the *Houqua*.[10]

Simon Bolivar, El Libertador. Courtesy of North Wind Photo Archives.

Russian Captain *Fabien Gottlieg von Bellinghausen*. Courtesy of Public Domain.

Alexander Smith Palmer portrait by Samuel Waldo. Courtesy of Historic Stonington.

Priscilla Denison Dixon Palmer. Courtesy of Historic Stonington.

Juliet Palmer Fanning portrait by Samuel Waldo.
Courtesy of Bradford Family private collection.

Sarah Fanning Bradford photograph. Courtesy of
Bradford Family Private Collection.

Eliza Babcock Palmer photograph. Courtesy of Historic
Stonington.

Nathaniel Brown Palmer II portrait by H. Allen Ross. Courtesy of Historic Stonington.

Edmund Fanning portrait. Courtesy of Bradford Family Private Collection.

Nathaniel sails his 47 ft Sloop *Hero* to Antarctica. Courtesy of Gerald B. Palmer

Hong Merchant Howqua portrait by George Chinnery. Courtesy of Public Domain.

Clipper Ship Houqua. Courtesy of Public Domain.

Currier and Ives print of *Great Republic*. Courtesy of Historic Stonington.

INSPIRER *and* MASTER *of* CLIPPER SHIPS *to* CHINA— *THE HOUQUA*

Captain Nathaniel Brown Palmer's final innovative role as a man of the sea would be to inspire a new approach to building ships for the lucrative trade which developed between China and the West. Working with the New York shipping firm of A.A. Low & Bros, he inspired a new design for what would be considered the first American clipper ship. His innovations in the *Houqua*, launched in May 1844, became a precursor for the even faster, more efficient clipper ships launched in succeeding years. These famous vessels designed by Americans such as John Griffiths and Donald McKay dominated the clipper ship trade between China, England, and the United States from 1845 until it declined in the late 1850s.[1]

Challenges faced the Low brothers and Captain Palmer when they began their ambitious efforts to trade with the Chinese in the early 1840s. The Portuguese had been the first western mariners to bring their goods to China. They arrived at Canton in 1516 and began their business by trading for silks and spices in a peaceful manner. When they began to rob and even kill the Chinese they were dealing with, this led the Chinese to begin setting some serious boundaries for western merchants trading with China.

China was a proud culture thousands of years old. The Chinese resented interference from foreign countries whose people they did not respect or even understand. They began to call the Portuguese "foreign devils." Eventually, the Chinese only allowed the Portuguese to trade and live in Macao, a tiny colony on the coast. Later, Macao became the base for the highly profitable international gambling center now visited by many Chinese and international gamblers.[2]

Captain Palmer and the Lows faced another historical challenge which had made the Chinese suspicious of foreign traders. By the early nineteenth century, English sea captains had begun to brazenly smuggle opium into China. Opium was easily available to them from the ports they had become familiar with in India. Making this destructive drug available to the Chinese people enraged Chinese government officials.

This posed another threat to China from foreigners. It led to the Opium War of 1842 between China and Great Britain, won by England's more powerful, better equipped naval fleet. The resulting Treaty of Nanking gave England the island of Hong Kong as a base for further trading with China, as well as access to the valuable trading areas China made available along its coast. China was also forced to pay Britain a huge indemnity of 21 million British pounds. Previously Houqua himself had paid the British $1.1 million dollars to lift their siege of Canton on the Pearl River. His fellow Chinese merchants contributed another $900,000. Next to Canton on the River was the principal area the Chinese had set aside for the British and Americans to set up establishments enabling them to trade with the Chinese merchants like Houqua.[3]

The Chinese forbade foreigners to enter the walled city of Canton, to have access to Chinese women, or even to learn the Chinese language. Foreign merchants were allowed, however, to establish their own communities nearby on the Pearl River. Here they developed extensive warehouses for their products, appropriate offices, and eventually communities for their western families.

Their success depended on the relationships they could establish with the Chinese traders appointed to deal with them. As the length of time they remained to do business with the Chinese increased, British and American merchants brought their families to live with them. They entertained each other with lavish dinners and had crew races between their different nationalities together on the Pearl River. Their families had to bring up their children and live in a culture that was not open to them.[4]

Foreign traders like Captain Palmer and the Lows were prohibited from docking their ships anywhere but Whampoa, twelve miles up the river from Canton. This is why times for the fastest voyage from China to London or New York and return often listed Whampoa as the port of departure or arrival. There were thousands of colorful Chinese vessels on the Pearl River, ranging from small sampans used for fishing to 500-ton junks with fierce eyes painted on their bows.

The variety of exotic Chinese foods, people in strange colorful dress, and other cultural differences must have dazzled the first Americans who came to China in the 1780s, much as they had dazzled their Portuguese and British predecessors years before. In the late eighteenth century, China had a population of 300 million compared to only about 2.5 million in America.[5]

A key advantage enjoyed by the European and American traders was the quality of the Chinese merchants with whom they worked. The merchants were capable, intelligent, honest men who dealt fairly with their foreign counterparts. They even tried to make the visitors and their families feel as welcome and comfortable as possible. The leading Chinese merchant was Houqua. He was then assumed to be one of the richest men in the world. Houqua had befriended the Lows before they first brought Nathaniel and Eliza to meet him in 1843.[6]

American entrepreneurs of the sea, most of whom were then based in New York like the Lows, included the shipping firm Howland & Aspinwall. They had begun to participate in the lucrative exchange of goods with China that was independent from the opium trade. When they learned the Chinese believed ginseng prolonged life, they began growing and gathering ginseng root in the northeast forests of New England to ship to China.

They added other products sought in China, such as seal fur skins and otter skins, sandalwood, manufactured cotton cloth, and exotic food products such as sea cucumbers, and shark fins. Silver coins, called "specie" was always welcomed in China, but it was limited in availability and Yankee traders had difficulty finding enough of it.[7]

The chief valuable product from China that enjoyed an insatiable market in both England and America was tea, in all of its exotic varieties available from the Canton merchants. Tea was a bulky product, requiring space below on the clipper ships transporting it. It also could spoil if stored too long, so speed in bringing it back to the western markets was important. Other Chinese products shipped to the west were its exotic oriental spices, such as gum Arabic, and musk. Later Chinese ceramics, or "Canton Ware," would enjoy a strong market in both Europe and the United States.

The first American ship to visit Canton was the *Empress of China,* captained by John Green in 1784. It took this vessel almost six months to reach China. Considering the time required to sell its cargo and reload, it was well over a year before it returned to New York. For the next sixty years, the roundtrip to Canton or Whampoa and return for English and American ships returning to London or New York would take up to a year. Ships that could make this trip with more speed and efficient cargo space were obviously required.[8]

Captain Palmer had gone into semi-retirement after completing his partnership with E.K. Collins in the packet ship trade with England during the 1830s. He was enjoying the opportunity in the early 1840s to spend more time at home with Eliza while traveling with her to New York and other cities. He was lured back to the sea to captain the *Paul Jones*, an American packet ship owned by R.B. Forbes from Boston. She sailed on her maiden voyage to Canton, China from Boston in January 1843 and returned to New York in October of that year.

Fatefully, one of his passengers was William Low of the prominent shipping firm A.A. Low & Bros. The firm had been founded by his older brother Abbott, who had begun to make a fortune in the China trade. It was a long, frustrating voyage. The *Paul Jones* was becalmed off Argentina for days. Up until this time, most of the vessels in the China trade were packet ships like the *Paul Jones*.[9]

Eliza sailed with husband Nathaniel on this, her first trip to China in 1843. She was put up by William Low's wife in their family compound on the Pearl River and even managed to meet Houqua himself. He gave Eliza his calling card, a four-inch square piece of red paper with his name in Chinese characters. He was as surprised by her pinched-in waist as the Americans were with Chinese women's bound feet.[10]

The relationship created between William Low and Captain Nathaniel Palmer on that voyage and their trip together back to America on the *Paul Jones* with their wives led to Nathaniel's involvement in the design and construction of the *Houqua*. On the return voyage to America William Low asked Nathaniel if he had an idea of how a better ship for the China trade could be designed and built. Captain Palmer took a block of wood and began to whittle it into a hull designed with a broader, flatter bottom as he had done for E.K. Collins's packet ships. William was convinced Nathaniel had made an important breakthrough with his concept for a new American clipper ship.[11]

Captain Palmer's concept would increase the speed of the new vessel, an important objective. The interior below would have more room for bulky cargos. The bow would be more streamlined. The new ships would not be designed to carry large numbers of passengers or packets of mail on scheduled routes like their predecessors, the British and American packets. Often their only passengers would be family members or friends of the captain.

Captain Palmer had thought out the entire concept of the distinct design for this new American vessel. He understood both English and American captains had been shipping opium to China from India, and his first idea was to build the new clipper on their models. On more reflection he decided to enlarge the dimensions of the carrying hold so it would be more suitable for tea than for opium. The Chinese Government's deep objection to western sea captains poisoning their people with shipments of opium from India had just led to the Opium War of 1842.

When William Low brought Captain Palmer to his older brother who had founded the family firm in New York, Abbot immediately approved Nathaniel's proposal and sent the plans for the new vessel to be constructed at the leading New York shipbuilders Brown & Bell. Abbott Low also decided to award Nathaniel with a 25 percent interest in the *Houqua*, an unusually large amount demonstrating how much he appreciated Captain Brown's contribution.[12]

American participation in the opium trade had been extensive since it was so profitable, and neither the American government nor its sea captains had turned away from this trade because of its moral implications and resistance from the Chinese Government. Nathaniel Palmer's shift from an emphasis on shipping opium to carrying tea was a trailblazing decision.[13]

The Lows and their new partner decided to honor the special attention they received from the great Chinese merchant Houqua by naming their first clipper after him. Nothing could have demonstrated his importance to the foreign trading community more than this symbolic act. Unfortunately Houqua died soon after their visit to him on September 4, 1843, nine months before the ship named for him was finally launched in New York, Friday, May 3, 1844.

The *Houqua* was also outfitted with bulwarks for sixteen guns and carried two cannons in case the Chinese might want to buy her for their Navy. They did not, and she sailed for many years in the China Trade.

When she was launched in New York, Abbot's younger brother Charles Low later wrote in his autobiography: "Captain N.B. Palmer had no superstition as to a Friday being a bad day to sail, though at that time sailors objected to going to sea on a Friday and many merchants were superstitious enough to wait for Saturday or even Sunday before they sent their ships to sea."[14]

James Gordon Bennet wrote in the *New York Tribune* on

Friday, May 3, 1844:

> She was one of the prettiest and most rakish looking
> clipper ships ever built in the civilized world …
> now to be seen at the foot of Jones' lane on the East
> River. … We never saw a vessel so perfect in all her
> parts. She is about 600 tons in size—as sharp as a
> cutter—as symmetrical as a yacht—as rakish in her
> rig as a pirate—and as neat in her deck and cabin
> arrangements as a lady's boudoir. …Her figure is a
> bust of Houqua, and her bows are as sharp as the
> toes of a pair of Chinese shoes.

Charles, "Charlie" Low went on to describe Captain Palmer from the point of view of a young crew member like himself:

> Captain Palmer was a rough old sailor. He was
> determined to see me get along, and helped me
> more than any other man to know my duty as an
> officer and eventually to fit me for a master. …Mr
> Hunt [First Mate] was a jolly fellow. Captain Palmer
> and Mr. Hunt got along splendidly and of course
> everything went off happily. …Captain Palmer
> was a believer in good feed, not alone only for the
> [Captain's] cabin; he believed in giving the sailors the
> very best of salt beef and pork and plenty of it; and
> everything else they had to eat was of the very best.[15]

On her maiden voyage to Canton on May 29, 1844, Nathaniel Palmer was Master, Thomas Hunt First Mate, William Gardner Second Mate, and Charles Low Third Mate. Several years later, Juliet Fanning's daughter, Sarah, would write a moving journal of her trip on the *Houqua* to China while traveling with Aunt Eliza and Uncle Nat as Master.

The *Houqua* was the precursor of the even faster ships that soon would constitute the zenith of the highly competitive clipper trade from 1844 until it declined in the 1850s. She made a voyage from New York to Hong Kong in eighty-four days, then the shortest time on record.

After the *Houqua* was launched the noted ship architect John Griffiths designed an improved clipper, the *Rainbow*, which was launched nine months later in February 1845. The *Rainbow* cost Howland & Aspinwall $45,000 compared to the *Houqua*'s modest $19,500. That indicates how profitable the investments of A.A. Low and Captain Palmer must have been. Even though the *Rainbow* became an advanced clipper, she never equaled the *Houqua*'s record for speedy voyages to China and back.

Griffiths followed her with the *Sea Witch*, a sharp-hulled vessel launched 2 &1/2 years after the *Houqua* in December 1846. She became the fastest clipper ship of all time, reaching New York from Canton in seventy-seven days, a record never equaled. This was a distance of 14,000 miles. It was deemed "The first true clipper." Nathaniel had never claimed that his ship was the final, best clipper model. He had simply shown the way for the great naval architects John Griffiths and Donald McKay to design and build even better clippers, which eventually included McKay's *Flying Cloud*.[16]

Later, at six years of age, the *Houqua* was still an effective vessel. This illustrates one of the key qualities that distinguished Captain Palmer's ships. They were built soundly of the best material to last, and they did, often sailing profitably for twenty years or more. In 1850, the *Houqua* made a run from Shanghai and back to New York in eighty-seven days, a record-breaking passage for the time. She remained efficient and seaworthy even though she had been remarkably reasonable to build.

When Nathaniel had first visited the A.A. Low offices in New York, the firm was relatively small, but ships like the *Houqua* made such great profits that they eventually created a fortune for the Low family. Seth Low, son of Abbott Low, was able to give Colombia University in New York a gift of one million dollars, an enormous sum at the time. Nathaniel reached the height of his prosperity as a partner with the Low Brothers. The *Houqua* continued to be a profitable ship in long haul trades until she was lost in a typhoon off Japan in 1865, more than twenty years after her launching.

Captain Palmer took the *Houqua* to Canton several times, but preferred to remain on his ship even though he was welcomed to stay on shore. Charlie Low continued in his story that: "The ships had to lie a long time in port, and after the rigging was overhauled and tarred down and all was painted aloft, the hull was painted inside and out, the deck was holystoned as white as snow, and then everything was kept in perfect order by Captain Palmer."[17]

By this time, Captain Nathaniel Brown Palmer had retired as an active sea captain, even though he continued to be a champion of American wooden sailing ships and to sponsor great American clippers like the *Oriental* with the Lows. His extensive work in so many key areas of the developing nineteenth-century shipping universe had made him a world respected, wealthy man. He had also shown the sea captains of his time how to compete with the English in the highly profitable blue-water trade with China.

CHAPTER 9

FAMILY TRAGEDIES—HOUSE FIRE, JULIET *and* PRISCILLA DIE PREMATURELY

IN THE LATE 1840S Nathaniel Brown Palmer and Eliza were living in a house built by his father outside the Stonington Borough called "Pine Point." Alex, his wife, Priscilla, and their four children had been living in Westerly, Rhode Island, near Priscilla's family, the Dixons. However by 1850 Alex and Priscilla either had just moved with their children completely into Pine Point with Nathaniel and Eliza or they had come there to live when Captain Palmer went on long voyages. Pine Point was built on a high piece of land on North Water Street. The area just across the street fronted on the eastern shore of Lambert (Quanaduck) Cove, which is now occupied by boat servicing operations. The substantial cove is at the inside end of Stonington Harbor.

The maid Frances was carrying a lighted candle as she climbed the staircase to her third-floor room at Pine Point in November 1850. A dress was hanging on the stairwell; she brushed the candle against it, and the building caught fire. The wooden house burned down to the ground. Nathaniel was away on a voyage to England at the time. Eliza wrote him a letter describing the tragedy. Younger brother Alex, Priscilla and their four children were living there with Eliza when the tragedy occurred.

November 26, 1850

My dear Husband,

I hope you have been carried safely across the
Atlantic, and that you are this day in Liverpool. I
was glad that the ship was seen on Sunday, for I have
seen that it was a boisterous night, and that a hard
gale followed. [Our home] is now a heap of ashes.
Oh, it is sad to be bereft of home and all its comforts
in the short hours [the fire took]. Yet many things
are spared, life, health, friends and with enough of
the worlds goods to make us comfortable. … But I
think it has learnt me a lesson not to lay up treasures
upon earth, and hoard up riches … which would
have done so much good, and which were scattered
to the winds. Dear Husband, what I regret most of
all is that I had a hundred dollars in the wardrobe,
and would not tell you of it. One reason was that
I meant to surprise you, or give it to the hundred
which Courtlandt owed you, and which I knew he
could not pay.
Then if I had done it your generous heart might have
felt as kindly toward him as mine does. … Many
things I miss very much-you too are a lover. But if
God will send the riches of his grace … we shall
praise him.
Alex thought he could sit down by his pleasant
fireside and take so much comfort. It is a great
disappointment, but still he is cheerful, and they all
behaved with admirable coolness and fortitude. Even
the children displayed wonderful presence of mind.
Natty [then 10] saved the basket of silver. Little
Libby [then 3] never cried and looked on in wonder.
Next day she saw your portrait and said:
"Uncle Nat bring Libby a new home." She tells

81

everybody: "Libby's house all burnt up." It's a
wonder Alex was not killed or suffocated, he was so
preserving, trying to save everything in the room.
… Alex's best clothes were saved fortunately, and
so were Priscilla's. "Now it seems clear Alex must
build," Someone said to him in Westerly. "Now you
will have to live here." Alex told him it would take
more than one fire to compel him to live there.

Hoping to hear from you in a fortnight and that you
may be preserved from every danger is the fervent
prayer of your affectionate wife, Eliza[1]

Nathaniel and Alex formerly had been planning to build
a larger, more modern house where they would live together
with their families. After the fire, they approached the architect
Gamaliel W. King, who had offices with a partner John Kellum
in Brooklyn and later in New York City. James Ingersoll Day,
son of Captain James Day of nearby New London, Connecticut,
had developed a substantial hardware business there. James was
building a house with King at the same time and offered advice
to the Palmer brothers in a letter of December 23, 1850, noting:
"Mine is probably a larger house than you would care to build
but its general arrangement could be worked into your plans. …
The inside finish I shall want of plain genteel style, nothing very
extravagant, probably such as you would adopt."[2]

The brothers went on to have a large, stately, Victorian mansion in
the Italianate style built for their families near the burned-out site of
Pine Point. They would live in it the rest of their lives. This splendid,
large white building on the hill is now called "The Palmer House."

Completed two years after the fire in 1852, it now houses the
offices of Historic Stonington (HS), and many of its portraits of
the Palmers, Stantons, Lopers and other local families. Beside
it in the 1990s, HS built its R.W. Woolworth Library to keep
its growing historical material on Stonington and surrounding
colonial towns.[3]

The first floor of the Palmer House has high ceilings and floor-to-ceiling windows with interior shutters. The house has fifteen rooms with eleven fireplaces and five chimneys. There are three stories with a spiral staircase leading up to a cupola, which has a fine view of Stonington Harbor and Lambert (Quanaduck) Cove.

Three of the important women in Nathaniel Palmer's extended family were his wife Eliza, his sister-in-law Priscilla Dixon Palmer, and his sister Juliet Palmer Fanning. They played an important role holding the Palmer-Stanton-Fanning families together when Nathaniel and Alex were captaining vessels all over the world.

After Nathaniel's friend William Fanning died prematurely of yellow fever in 1826 in the West Indies, sister Juliet was left a widow at only eighteen years of age. She became an active correspondent, keeping family members informed of each other's activities in the Palmer-Stanton-Fanning families. Brothers Charles and Joseph Stanton had married three of her sisters. Charles first married Ann Adelaide, and when she died, younger sister Nancy. Joseph married sister Grace.

After William died, Juliet and her one-year-old daughter, Sarah, lived with her father-in-law, Captain Edmund Fanning, and his wife, Sarah. When daughter Sarah came into her teens, Juliet received sufficient support from Edmund to travel extensively, visiting family members and friends in Albany, New Orleans, and other locations. The Fanning grandparents were devoted to Sarah.

Juliet sent Sarah to a private school near New York City. A precocious, well-educated girl, Sarah later kept fascinating journals while traveling with her mother and later in 1848 sailing with Eliza and Nathaniel on the clipper ship *Houqua* back and forth to China.

Juliet's letter to her seventeen-year-old daughter, Sarah, soon after Sarah's grandparents had died within a week of each other demonstrates how the Palmer women used their deep belief in God, not only to take them though the sad periods of life's disappointments, but especially to teach their children how to live like Christians:

February 4, 1842, New York

My dear Child,

You must learn to control your feelings to discipline
your mind and to have faith to trust in God. If you
believe and act accordingly, that when he sends you
trouble, he will also send the comforter…through
Christ, who was himself a man of sorrow and
acquainted with grief.
God saw fit to take your grandparents together. They
could not be separated; they have lived beyond the
age allotted to man. We have everything to comfort
us in their death. They were honored and respected
in life, in death lamented, and left behind pure and
unspotted names.

Your mother, Juliet[4]

Juliet was an attractive young widow. She had a number of
admirers after her husband, William, died in 1826 but preferred
to remain single. Sister Grace and her husband, Joseph Warren
Stanton, often invited Juliet to visit them in New Orleans:

February 17, 1840

My dear Sister [Juliet],

The gallant Captain Nathaniel Palmer Durfey, dined
with us yesterday and the health of Absent friends
was drunk, and especial mention made of yourself;
he agreed that, provided that we could persuade
you to make a visit this spring, he would esteem it a
privilege to take charge of you and more especially
that your passage would be free. It will be a great
comfort to Grace since she is much alone. We are

already promising ourselves the special pleasure of
having you with us. …You will meet many friends
and acquaintances here & we promise to give you
plenty of Gumbo. You will enjoy it. Our Pastor is
a great speaker. …We have often said: "how Juliet
would enjoy this or that sermon." …
Give love to Sarah & our parents.

Yours affectionately, J.W. Stanton[5]

Several years later, on November 1, 1844, Juliet and her
daughter Sarah, now eighteen, took another trip to New Orleans
to see sister-aunt Grace and other family members. They had a
wonderful time visiting with family and friends in New Orleans.
This would be Juliet's last journey.

The last months of Juliet's life are described in Sarah's Journals
of November 1844–1845. They provide a day-by-day description
of her trip to the mouth of the Mississippi, followed by a voyage
on a steamboat up the great river accompanied by Aunt Grace.
They followed this with a voyage on the Great Lakes, after
which they returned by stagecoach to New York City. During
the journey, Juliet came down with a threatening disease while
in New Orleans. Many serious illnesses could not be effectively
identified or treated by the medical assistance available in mid-
nineteenth-century America.[6]

Sarah indicates her mother became sick on May 16, 1845,
before they left New Orleans to sail up the Mississippi: She wrote,
"Mother's face is badly swollen, she is not getting better".[7]

On July 9, they began their trip by steamer. They passed St.
Louis and went on to the Indian country in the upper middle
west. Sarah shares her vivid observations of the Indians of the
plains-the Sacs, Foxes, and Sioux, providing a colorful report of
the journey through mid-nineteenth-century America

It seems to be a dream sailing among the Indian
lands and hearing their wars and hunting grounds

spoken of as a thing of today. A Mr R. Says in the last great [Indian] battle he slept eight miles from the battleground. …[H]e saw one Indian eat a piece of the heart of an enemy chief roasted on a piece of stick. When one party conquered the other, they dressed their dead enemies in the war garments and sealed them under a tree with all their weapons. … Saw more Indians in canoes. …The women were very fine looking—such splendid teeth. Had their faces painted red and where the hair was parted, a red streak went up like blood. …Their marriage ceremony is very singular and simple. The man calls together all his relations and friends and tells them he wishes to be married. They all bring him presents, such as blankets, horses knives etc, which he carries and places by the door of his love's wigwam. If she intends to accept his addresses, she takes the presents and distributes them among her brothers and sisters. Then her family gives a feast and invites the man & his friends and he takes the girl on the back of his horse and trots off home with her, and thus they are married. If the girl does not accept she leaves the gifts untouched.

Her mother's health worsens:

August 6, 1845—Mother was taken quite sick. Woman in a log cabin gave her Whiskey, she had a chill and the liquor made her deathly. Was so glad to get to Janesville, Wisconsin & put her to bed. Was alarmed by the omen of a beautiful cloud, looking like a person carved out. It gradually faded away like a person dying.

On August 8, 1845, they left Milwaukee on a Great Lakes Steamer the *Missouri* bound for Buffalo. Sunday, August 10, they arrived in Detroit. "Mother was sick all day, could keep nothing on her stomach." Sunday, August 17, they finally arrived in New York: "Dr Gray says Mother is very sick."

Juliet Palmer Fanning died at the Astor House in New York City on August 23, 1845, at the age of thirty-seven. Her death records state that she died of Congestive Fever. This was defined in the *Concise Genealogical Dictionary* by Maureen and Glenn Harris, *Ancestry*, Salt Lake City as "malaria."[8]

Sarah's journal:

> All is over and I am Motherless. Oh! The agony
> condensed in that one word. … My beloved Mother,
> would God that I had died with thee, my Mother.
> … A man can grow, can make himself an aim.
> Ambition can fill his soul, but a woman's ambition
> lies in her affections, as Longfellow writes. … But
> God alone knows the agony I experience at the
> thought that it may be years before I can ever see her
> face. Oh! My Mother, how I long to see, to embrace
> you. My soul yearns for thy kind loving looks.[9]

After her mother's death, Sarah went on writing to her extended family, and lived an astonishing ninety-four years until her death in 1919. Three years after Juliet passed in 1848, Sarah married Edward Bradford from Plainfield, Connecticut, whom she had met in New Orleans. Their marriage was celebrated at Trinity Church in New York, and they eventually had nine children together. Only two of Sarah and Edward's nine children lived to maturity. Mortality was always present for nineteenth-century families.

To cheer this spirited, intelligent girl up after the recent loss of her mother, Eliza and Nathaniel invited Sarah to be their guest on a voyage of the *Houqua* to China. It left New York on April 4, 1846, having just arrived in New York from Canton with a cargo of tea. Sarah's journal of that trip displays her keen observations in selected quotes:

Left the Astor at 12 and proceeded on the steamer
which conveyed us to the good ship Houqua.
Uncle Nath says I am his baby, he does love me
and I am ungrateful not to feel it more. I will
strive for a better frame of mind. Mother, dear
Mother how I miss you. You would have enjoyed
this voyage so much! Love can fly away, or those
who are taken from us and we are left in misery,
but knowledge once gained is ours forever. What
consoles us like books?
Several vessels passed us. Spoke with two. How
ingenuous is man! To think that conversation can
be carried on at a distance of miles by pieces of
cloth sewed together into a flag! One ship came so
near that Uncle Nath used the speaking trumpet.
"Where from?" Shouted he. "Isle of France!"
"Where bound?" "London". They then asked us.
"Houqua from New York to Canton" screamed
Uncle Nath. We signaled another ship. Oh they did
look so beautiful. The water and sky were of a deep
blue and the ships riding off with their white sails.
Just enough sea to cause them to bend gracefully to
the breeze. It seemed as if the ships were bowing to
each other as they neared.
Tonight, Uncle Nath sent two bottles of "grog" to
the men to encourage them in their preparation
for Neptune's appearance [Crossing the Equator].
There was one who "fiddles" finely. The crew
danced. The dancers had cigars in their mouths
and, we could only see the light of their cigars
flying in and out through the rigging, and hear the
feet stomping in time. I wanted to join the dancers
but did not. What sea with pleasant weather and
a good ship can do for us. A Rovers life for me!
After that Uncle Nat gave Aunt Eliza and me a
fine shower bath.[10]

The second tragic loss by premature death in Nathaniel Palmer's greater family occurred when Priscilla, Alex's loving wife and Eliza's close friend, died at age thirty-six on January 12, 1851. She left four children: Natty, 10; Alexander, 7; Louis Lambert, 5; and Elisabeth ("Libby"), 2 & 1/2.

Eliza writes Nathaniel about the tragedy:

Tuesday Evening, January 13, 1851

My dear Husband,

I know your heart has been with the sorrowing
family today, as they convened there, and one, dear
Priscilla to the tomb… Alex said: "Can you realize
we shall never see Priscilla any more", and he took
little Libby in his arms and said: "Where is dear
Mama?" Oh it was a sad sight to see him take his
three little boys to their mother's funeral. How
gratified Priscilla would have been to have seen them.
She spoke of you many times and she said she loved
you. You had been a good brother to her and that
you must prepare to meet her, she forgot no one and
I'm sure her prayer will be answered. I'm so glad I
came as she knew me, called me by name and kissed
me and then her mind wandered again. It was the
most disturbing scene I ever witnessed … but let
us determine dear husband with the help of God to
meet her and all the departed ones who have gone.

Good bye, your Eliza[11]

Older brother Nathaniel was not able to get back to Stonington in time to be with Priscilla before she died or for her funeral. However, the day after her death, he wrote his brother Alex a letter expressing that he and Eliza would help bring up the children for the rest of their lives.

January 13, 1851

Dear Brother,

Overwhelmed with sorrow, I sit down to write a
few lines-hoping to mitigate if possible some of the
accumulated sorrow which of late have been heaped
upon you…you have my hearty cooperation in
bringing up the three children for I will leave you
no more. We have enough of the world's goods to
educate your children & to make us comfortable the
residue of our days.

Your devoted brother, Nathaniel Palmer[12]

Nathaniel, Eliza, and Alex went on to build the house they
had been building for both of their families after a fire destroyed
Pine Point. The spacious home facing Lambert (Quanaduck)
Cove, was completed within two years in 1852. Alex and his four
children lived there after Priscilla died until the children grew up
and ventured out to become adults decades later. Nathaniel and
Eliza lived there together for the rest of their lives. In the early
1850s they began to help brother Alex bring up nephews Natty,
Alex, and Louis Lambert and niece Libby in Stonington.

CHAPTER 10

CAPTAIN PALMER'S SWAN SONG
—CHAMPION *of* AMERICAN WOODEN SAIL

BEFORE THE PALMER FAMILY lost PRISCILLA in January 1851, Nathaniel Brown Palmer had decided to retire from being an active sea captain. He was worn out by the challenges of captaining vessels at sea and tired of being away from Eliza, relatives, and friends in Stonington and New York, the two places where he began to spend more of his time.

Nathaniel had made enough money so he and Eliza could do as they pleased while enjoying his well-earned reputation. On June 7, 1845, the year after the Club was founded, he had become an early member of the New York Yacht Club. He and Eliza were welcomed in port cities they visited all over the world. Meanwhile they continued to help Alex bring up his four children at their shared house in Stonington. From the 1850s on they had more time to visit family in New Orleans and other American cities.

After he made his last voyage as an active sea captain in 1849, Nathaniel spent the next few years partnering with the Low family working on the design and construction of three great American wooden clipper ships: 1) The *Oriental* (1849); 2) The *N.B. Palmer* (1851); and 3) The *Contest* (1852). He received ownership shares in each of them. He also acted as a personal champion for American wooden ships of sail in the mid-1850s when they began to be challenged by the new steam driven, ironclad ships made in England. America's expert on the clipper era, Arthur H. Clark commented: "Few men in private life have had part of a continent, a great clipper ship and a yacht [schooner-yacht *Palmer*] named after them."[1]

The audience Captain Nathaniel Palmer was determined to impress with these memorable American clippers were the English ship owners, builders and the British Admiralty who reigned as the world's dominant maritime players of the nineteenth century. They were often present at the London and Liverpool docks when the clippers he had inspired came into port in the early 1850s from China, or American ports like New York.

When the English press covered the *Oriental*'s arrival at the Liverpool docks in 1850, Captain Palmer was there to welcome her along with crowds of English supporters. Here are the newspaper reports from the *London Times*, according to Arthur Clark:

> "The first American ship to carry a cargo of tea
> from China to England after the repeal of the
> Navigation Laws was the clipper *Oriental*, of 1003
> tons....She sailed from New York on her first voyage,
> commanded by Captain N.B. Palmer, September 14,
> 1849, and arrived at Hong Kong in 109 days. This
> was Captain's Palmer's last command.

> "The *Oriental* sailed on her second voyage from New
> York for China, May 19, 1850 under the command
> of Captain Theodore Palmer, a younger brother of
> Captain Nat…She arrived at Hong Kong…and
> chartered to load tea for London at L6 per ton of 40
> cubic feet, while British ships were waiting there for
> cargos to London at L3:10 per ton of 50 cubic feet.
> She arrived at London's West India Docks in 97
> days from Hong Kong-a passage from China never
> equaled in point of speed.

> "No ship like the *Oriental* ever had ever been
> seen in England, and the ship owners of London

were constrained to admit they had nothing to
compare with her in speed, beauty of model, rig, or
construction…The arrival of this vessel in London
…aroused as much appreciation and excitement in
Great Britain as was created by the memorable Tea
Party held in Boston harbor in 1773." The *London
Times* went on: "We must not be beat. We trust that
our countrymen will not be beaten, but if they are,
we shall know that they deserve it."[2]

What a sensation Captain Palmer and his partners the Lows
had created in England with their clipper *Oriental.* By appointing
Theodore Palmer, Captain of the *Oriental* at age thirty-three, and
then encouraging his younger sibling by seventeen years to make
the best possible time on his first voyage from Hong Kong to
London, he assured his younger brothers would become first rate
sea captains like himself. Nathaniel reported his younger brother
had been received "like a lion" in England. Justifiably proud, He
had shifted from building his own reputation to advancing the
careers of his younger mentees.

Brother Theodore retired from blue water sailing after
captaining one more trip on the *Oriental* in 1852. He returned
to Stonington where he married Harriet Billings on October 25,
1853. He died in 1865 at forty-nine years of age, fourteen years
after making his lauded journey as Captain of the *Oriental* from
Hong Kong to London. He had been suffering from "softening of
the brain," or parietal disease.

While Theodore struggled with the disease that affected his
brain, brothers Nathaniel and Alex did all they could to help him
and his family through the following difficult years. On January
18, 1863, Nathaniel wrote a letter to Alex describing how they
had been struggling to resolve Theodore's disturbed financial
affairs. The older brothers went so far as to pay his bills, perhaps
sometimes with their own money. They had tried in vain to get
some key papers from Theodore's wife, Harriet, who refused to
provide them:

January 18, 1863

Dear Brother

I note what you note in regard to Theodore's affairs.
I think you had better get receipts-Theo D. Palmer
Jr, NB Palmer attorney-I would pay all bills, duly
rendered, by the parties in whom due, scrutinizing
them closely and demanding bond—when
necessary…I have collected some dividends…I shall
order all to be collected and deposited to his credit.
I spoke to Nathan about it coming down, I said to
him she [Harriet] refused to give me the papers. He
replied he did not know how he could compel her
to do so. So I concluded to grab all I can get hold
of and compel her to be the assailant. Get hold of
Theo when he is straight in his mind & see if he has
any recollection of what he has in his box and try to
remember yourself if there were any other valuable
papers except the bond in question.
Libby & Willie and Master Theodore [Children of
brother William Lord Palmer] came and dined with
me Tuesday.

Give love to all, Your affectionate brother, NB Palmer

After Theodore's death on January 15, 1865, in Stonington, his widow, Harriet, moved with their sons to Easthampton, Massachusetts, where she lived for the rest of her life. She died of "softening of the brain" on December 16, 1876.[3]

The second great American clipper designed and built for Nathaniel and the Lows at that time was the *N.B. Palmer*. This was the largest of his clippers at 214 feet long, thirty-nine feet broad, and twenty-two feet deep measuring 1,490 tons.

Arthur Clark wrote:

"The *N.B. Palmer* was perhaps the most famous
ship built in the Westervelt Yard [Jacob Westervelt
had been Mayor of New York City]. In China she
was known as "the Yacht" and with her nettings
in the tops, brass guns, gold stripe, and her lavish
entertainment on the fourth of July and Washington's
Birthday she deserved that title…A full rigged model
of the N.B. Palmer was exhibited at the Crystal Place
in London in 1851 and attracted much attention as a
fine example of the American clipper type.[4]

The *N.B. Palmer* was captained by the same Charlie Low whom
Captain Palmer had taken on board the *Houqua* as his third mate
seven years before. Nathaniel Palmer was continuing his new role
as sponsor of young captains. Charlie had been taught by him to
be a responsible seaman, an able mate, and eventually a captain
himself. He was also recognizing his deep debt to the Lows by his
special attention to their younger brother.

Charlie continued as master of the *N.B. Palmer* for the next
several years. He must have been influenced by Captain Palmer's
practice of taking his wife Eliza along on long voyages before that
practice was common. Charlie's young wife Sally became known
as an attractive, charming lady. She was sought after in leading
social circles in the ports where Charlie docked the *N.B. Palmer*.[5]

The third large wooden clipper under sail sponsored by
Nathaniel and the Lows in the early 1850s was the *Contest*. As
an example of the value Nathaniel obtained for his participation
with the Lows in the design and construction of these clippers, he
received four shares in the *Contest,* a 9 percent ownership interest.

The ship measured 1,098 tons and was a fine racer. Her record
on the run from New York to San Francisco was ninety-seven days,
the same as John Griffith's *Sea Witch*. The *Contest* was captured ten
years later by Captain Raphael Semmes of the Confederate cruiser
Alabama on November 11, 1863, during the American Civil War.
Spears quotes Captain Semmes's report of his chase, capture, and
burning of the *Conquest*. The *Alabama,* Semmes's famous ironclad,

sail-and-steam-powered raider, had sighted the *Conquest* off Java. She was returning to New York from Yokohama with Japanese trade goods for the northern American markets.

> "When the captain was brought on board, I congratulated him on the skillful handling of his ship, and expressed my admiration of her fine qualities. He told me she was one of the most famous clipper ships out of New York. I was sorry to be obliged to burn this beautiful ship and regretted much that I had no armament for her so that I might commission her as a cruiser. She was the *Contest,* from Yokohama in Japan, bound to New York. She was light, and in fine sailing trim, having only a partial cargo on board. There being no attempt to cover the cargo, consisting mostly of light Japanese goods…I condemned both ship and cargo.[6]

Years later, the claim against the Confederacy for destruction of the *Contest* was settled by the Geneva Board of Arbitration in 1876. The lawyer representing the ship's owners obtained a payment of about $67,000. This was Abbot Low, Nathaniel Palmer's partner and original financier of the *Houqua.* The *Contest* had been the most expensive clipper ship they had ever built at $95,000. Her cost was justified since her first cargo had netted $48,000 and she was afloat for twelve years before being captured. Semmes valued the prize at $122,815. The American claim was $158,465. After deductions the owners actually received only $47,465 from the Geneva Board some twelve years after her capture and sinking. Nathaniel's share of the payment after legal and other costs was $6,000, and he was still alive to receive it.[7]

Captain Palmer's involvement with the *Great Republic* provides the last example of his belief that wooden sailing ships would continue to prevail, compared to the new ironclad, steam, propeller driven ships being built in England. Just after she was built in Boston and was being finally outfitted in New York, the

Great Republic's tar treated lines and sails were consumed in a terrible fire on December 26, 1853. It was just before she was about to sail for London. Heroic efforts from local New York fire companies could not save her and the fire went into the hull. She went to the bottom beside the dock, having been abandoned by her owners.

The *Great Republic* was the largest wooden ship ever launched. Her famous designer, Donald McKay, king of the clipper ship architects, had an interest in her. McKay had tried to save her in vain; he was in despair. Captain Palmer was there and ran into his friend, who said he was going to write her off at a total loss. Nathaniel said: "I'll buy her from you, Donald." McKay looked at him is stunned disbelief. "You're daft man! She's worthless. Why? So I won't be ruined? Is that it?" Palmer shook his head. "No because I believe in her. Because I believe in you, Donald. The *Great Republic* will sail again."[8]

Nathaniel had promised Donald MaKay that A.A. Low and Brothers would buy the *Great Republic* from McKay when she was lying at the bottom beside the pier in New York without checking before with any of the Low partners. The Lows had complete confidence in his judgment and immediately approved his offer. They went on to have the *Great Republic* rebuilt, without her original upper deck, at a total cost of only $27,000. In her new form, the *Great Republic* was still much larger than any ship of the sail afloat. She measured 3,355 tons and had a capacity of more than 4,000 tons.[9]

Captain Palmer saved the original figurehead of the ship, a beautiful carved head of an eagle covered with gold leaf, and took it back to his home in Stonington. It is now displayed in the Mystic Seaport Museum.

He sent the rebuilt *Great Republic* to London February 21, 1855, where she was consigned to W.S. Lindsay, a London firm of the highest standing. She was subsequently purchased by the French government and used to transport troops during the Crimean War against Russia.

The British were beginning to turn the tide by making

more efficient steam-powered ships clad with iron. By 1860, they eventually made the formerly dominant U.S. clipper ships obsolete. During the mid-1850s American shipbuilders continued to use wood for the hull while the British used iron, and the Americans utilized paddle wheels, while the British also adopted the screw propeller.[10]

Captain Palmer had earned a reputation with the British Admiralty and leading maritime players there as an authoritative American voice. They often came to see him during his visits to England. Nathaniel continued to argue that sail was still better than steam and that properly built wood hulls were still better than iron. Nevertheless, the British became convinced the new concepts of ship construction would prevail.

As a last hurrah, Captain Palmer had been invited by shipbuilders and owners in Liverpool to make his case for the wooden ships of sail. The English were talking about the development of their new iron ships as they stood in front of one of them in the shipyard. Captain Palmer challenged them. He had brought a musket with him and said he could fire its ball through the hull. They made a wager and he won it by firing the ball through the iron surface.[11]

But his colorful performance made no difference. The Americans were slow to understand that their wooden, sail driven ships would soon be surpassed and outdated by the British ironclad, steam and propeller driven vessels that became superior in terms of both speed and dependability. They would not be as limited by the vicissitudes of wind or weather that could plague the performance of the great American clippers.

Despite the trend towards the new ships which began to be built in England at this time, American wooden clipper ships of sail were still immensely popular in America. The building of clipper ships in the United States reached its height in 1853. That year forty-eight clippers were added to the California fleet, and the excitement of building, owning, and racing them reached its peak. Many Americans who had capital to invest wanted to own or invest in a clipper. The ship building yards were taxed to their capacity, and captains, officers, and crews for such a large number of vessels were hard to find.[12]

The term "California clipper" used at that time referred to the large number of clippers that went back and forth from Boston or New York to San Francisco beginning in the California gold rush. In 1854, for example, these ships made twenty passages from the Atlantic port to San Francisco in 110 days or less, a very fast voyage. Much attention was given by the press to these races and wagers on California Clippers trying to better each other's times.

However, in 1856 the American merchant marine began to decline in its tonnage carried compared to that of foreign countries. It went from 65,000 tons in 1855 to 17,000 tons in 1860, a reduction of 75 percent. The tonnage of the vessels themselves built in the United States went from 583,450 tons in 1855 to 378,804 tons in 1857. Beginning in the late 1860s the American shipbuilders finally began to turn their attention to building the new ironclad steam driven vessels.[13] The Americans resisted changing from wood and sail and from the paddle wheel to iron-clad ships driven by steam and the screw propeller until the bitter end.

Captain Nathaniel Brown Palmer had persisted in doing his best to defend the wooden sailing ships he had sailed, overcoming every imaginable challenge, over the past forty years. It was time for the American master mariner to retire from his struggles on the seas.

CHAPTER 11

THE GOLDEN YEARS

It is not unusual for those under financial pressure to turn to their successful greater family members in time of need. The extended Palmer family was no exception. In 1855 an appeal for funds was made to Nathaniel Brown Palmer by sister Grace's husband, Joseph Warren Stanton. Its tone indicated not only that Joseph was confident he would help them out but also that other family members sometimes made similar requests of him. This is indicated from the confident way Joseph describes how Nathaniel should make the funds available:

> New Orleans, August 10, 1855
>
> Brother Nathaniel,
>
> To reach the fall business season, we wish to finance
> by your aid and have enclosed our two drafts
> amounting to $9,550 for your acceptance. I have
> left the date and time open in order to meet the
> requirements of parties who purchase. We shall
> only need to reach the coming business season, and
> therefore shall not wish to extend them. Please make
> them payable at a Bank or at the office of A.A. Low
> & Bros.
> The insurance office that is upon the *A Celt* [a
> sunken ship] is still engaged in trying to raise her.

they will pay us when satisfied in trying, having
spent already nearly $10,000.

Grace William and myself are quite well.
Yours truly J.W. Stanton[1]

One of Nathaniel's favorite young Palmers was his namesake
"Natty," Alex and Priscilla's oldest son. He took a particular
interest in the boy's education and followed his development.
The schooling available to young people in Stonington had
improved over the first half of the nineteenth century. In
1858 Natty wrote a remarkable essay on immigration which
illustrated the development in education available to children
from the sea faring Stonington families.

In a letter from London on January 22, 1858, Uncle Nathaniel
had encouraged Natty to get the best education possible, noting
he felt the lack of getting enough proper schooling himself:

I am delighted to hear you are pursuing your
studies so steadily & I hope profitably. Now is the
time for you to improve your mind & to bring it
under subjection to discipline, the want of which
your uncle "Nat" feels the deficiency of in everyday
disclosures & in the voyage of life & had I done as
my kind father & mother wished me to do.[2]

Nathaniel closely followed the boy's schoolwork. Natty
became a good writer but hadn't had an opportunity to learn
much about the world. This is where his Uncle Nathaniel could
help. Given the understanding of European events driving
immigration and the current role of immigrants in America
demonstrated in Natty's essay, we surmise Nathaniel helped
him write the essay when father Alex, was far away at sea.

Here is Natty's essay, written in the Spring of 1858 when he
was seventeen years old:

Ought Immigration To Be Encouraged?

In supporting the affirmative of this question we shall first present the claims of justice: for in every dispute justice is the final judge. Nine tenths of all who immigrate to our shores are those who fled from the yoke of foreign despotism. They come to America because it is "the land of the free", "an asylum for the oppressed", and here they find relief and protection from tyranny.
We have a national debt of three or four millions of dollars which hangs as a dark prospect over us every hour increasing the price of our food, diminishing our daily gains. How shall we escape from this burden? There is only one way. Capitalist speculators, brokers cannot pay the debt, for they do not increase the national wealth.
The laboring man on the other hand is continually swelling the public treasury. Every pair of boots made, every manufacturer adds to the value of our public capital. … It is sound policy then for us to welcome to America every "honest son of toil".
But you say, Immigrants are inferior to Americans. We grant it, but it is universally conceded that after the third generation, becoming acclimated and naturalized, they lose this inferiority and are as good as the best of us.

Nathaniel Palmer II[3]

Nathaniel Palmer was a wise man who deeply understood how the world worked. It was in this mode that he helped everyone around him better understand what to do with their lives. He expected the Palmer children to write down and act on his guidance.

Another theme that emerges in the family correspondence during his retirement years is the American Civil War which waged from 1861 to 1865. Here is a letter from Joseph Warren Stanton, Grace's husband, written to Natty from The Willard Hotel in Washington, D.C. in the last year of the conflict. Natty was then twenty-four years old, working in a factory in Stonington making firearms. He never became a sea captain like his father and uncle.

It is understandable that Joseph Stanton strongly supported the views of the Confederacy, since he had been living in Louisiana, one of the original Southern Secession States, for many years.

Willard's Hotel, Washington, November 9, 1864

Dear Nathaniel,

Between nine and ten O'clock last night, by the use
of magnetism, it was announced here that Lincoln
was elected President, for another term of 4 years!
This is a consummation of Abolition Views &
exertions, and they have been riotously rejoicing,
through all the balance of the night; and doubtless
Satan and his Satellites are glorying in the triumph!
There was rejoicing at the Crucifixion, but the
event turned the war of destruction, upon the very
perpetrators.No war feelings will be softened in the
North, and the South viewing nothing but utter
destruction before them, will like the rat, when
cornered, first squeal, then turn and fiercely attack
the enemy!!!
At all events New England will have "killed the
goose that laid the golden egg". Her navigation
is rubbed out; and her manufactures are sure to
come into competition that no power can enable
her to understand! I am sorry for this. I am a New
Englander, but I could not uphold error for the
nearest friend on earth. God is truth and I stand for
his character against all the earth!

Destroy this when read, or let none see it but your
father, who feels as I do.

Yours truly, J.W. Stanton[4]

Natty's father, Alex, may have been the only Palmer in the
North who shared Joseph Stanton's views about the Civil War.
In an earlier letter of March 11, 1864, written to his niece
Sarah in France, where she gone from New Orleans to escape
the dangers of the Civil War, Alex described a note he had just
received from his sister Grace concerning the death of a young
Confederate soldier Sarah had known:

> Grace came in last evening [by letter] for the first
> time since I wrote you. She felt bad on hearing of
> the death of your friend, it caused her to denounce
> the men who are in power destroying their country,
> she was very severe & bitter at the destruction in
> Louisiana. …
> We have no positive news from N Orleans for a
> week. Every move this spring by Northern troops has
> failed of success, while the administration is more
> anxious to perpetuate their power; next fall the ultras
> [will be] howling after the Negro.[5]

In 1872 Nathaniel Palmer wrote a letter to Natty's brother,
Louis Lambert Palmer, indicating he could be firm but fair with
relatives who borrowed money from him for their ventures that
didn't always work out. Louis may have made a few troubled
investments, hence his uncle's jocular use of the phrase: "if I
was not so poor." Nathaniel indicated Louis's sister Libby, then
twenty-four, was still living in the big house when its garden
flourished in late spring.

Stonington, June 19, 1872

Dear Lambert,

Yours of the 24th came to hand this morning & you must have misconstrued my letter in relation to the compounded interest on "Nat's loan" & if I were not so poor, you would never have heard from me on the subject, but I never claimed there was due, more interest than I call'd for, half yearly at the amt you sent. One year's interest was re'd here.I am quite busy now having the house painted. … Libby's Room is finished, and some outside work done on the Barn and outhouses. Then also the *Sallie* [Nathaniel's yacht] is hauled out, & is having a general overhaul, scraping and painting etc to be put in first rate order. Have heard nothing from your Father since the 29th April in Florence. I suppose they must be in France or England. Thinking about putting their faces homeward about these days. I hope they will hurry up

Your affectionate Uncle, N.b. Palmer

Please acknowledge the receipt of your draft.[6]

In the years after his retirement, Nathaniel Palmer modeled and owned seventeen yachts at different times, including the *Sallie*. He sailed them with family and friends from the New York Yacht Club. With Eliza and one of the young Palmers, such as Natty or Sarah, he continued to occasionally make long voyages to England or China, where he was welcomed by his mariner friends in each country. Sometimes he would travel alone to be on hand when one of his protegees, such as younger brother Theodore or Charlie Low, was captaining one of his clipper ships sailing to London, Liverpool, or Canton. He had become a citizen of the world and enjoyed visiting it. His brother Alex wrote: "Capt. Nat's home was the whole world. He had friends everywhere and was perfectly at home wherever he went."[7]

Nathaniel, who had always been an avid fisherman and hunter, now joined the sportsmen who belonged to the famous Currituck Club, which had extensive shooting areas for both water and other birds in North Carolina. He became a director of entities such as the *Fall River* line of steamers and helped build the steamers *Providence* and *Bristol*. He lost some money when investing in the *Neptune* line with William S. Williams. This was not unusual. Like other men who amassed considerable wealth, in retirement he was lured onto many ventures. Some worked out, others did not.

Nathaniel Brown Palmer's beloved wife, Eliza, died in 1872 at the age of sixty-two, breaking his heart. Ever since he married her as a girl of sixteen in 1826, she had been the anchor of his life and the centerpiece of his extended Palmer family. By then Nathaniel may have realized how difficult it must have been for Eliza to deal with his absence for years at sea. Like his brother Alex, he never married again after losing Eliza.

In his grief about her, Nathaniel wrote a letter to his nephew, Lambert Palmer, when Lambert was practicing law in Chicago:

May 13, 1872

Dear Lambert,

I was right glad to hear you are well & busy in your profession. Now is the time to make hay—in the days of your youth. ...I am very lonely living with your Uncle William [Nat's brother William Lord Palmer] who with your aunt Sallie are very kind to make me comfortable, but I miss your aunt Eliza so much—her sickness & death seem like a dream. I can't seem to get over the reality. I go up and wander about the house. Everything remains the same but your aunt Eliza who is absent & forever—which is a crushing fact and one hard to get over ...

Your affectionate uncle N.B. Palmer[8]

After Nathaniel lost Eliza, family members like brother Alex
kept a close watch on him as his capacities began to dwindle. Alex
wrote him a year after his loss:

Dear Nat, April, 1873

Last Sunday we passed the day with George, Captain
Cobb was with us part of the time. Your name was
often mentioned, and many conjectures were made
as regards your health. If you were really improving,
and how soon you would be fit for active duty. How
are you feeling Nat, please state, not what the Doc
says—we know what he would say, but how you feel
yourself, whether you are feeling stronger, and can
endure more fatigue, also as regards your weight, and
the fistula, whether it is kept open or not. Let us hear
just how you are …
From your affect brother,

Alex Palmer[9]

Nathaniel's brother Alexander Palmer continued his
distinguished career after retiring from being an active sea captain
in the 1850s. For many years he served as a member of the
Connecticut General Assembly as a State Senator. Alex was known
in his later years as a modest man. He kept in close touch with
his four children-Natty, Alexander, Louis Lambert, and Libby,
and his three sisters and their husbands. Alex never remarried after
losing Priscilla in 1851. During his long well deserved retirement
period he was often honored for his dedication to his family, to his
community, and to his maritime brothers.[10]

Nathaniel Palmer and his nephew became even closer after
Eliza died, leaving him alone. Natty's varied career began at the
hardware store Bruff Bros & Seaver in New York. He went on to
be head salesman of a branch they established in New Orleans,
where his aunt Grace was living with her husband Joseph Stanton.

The Civil War was about to begin. Natty wrote letters to his father, Alex, in Stonington describing the mobilization of the Confederacy and excitement when it attacked Fort Sumter in Charleston, South Carolina.

Alex wrote back noting he was happy his son had not joined a Confederate military unit, but expressed concern that Natty was still in New Orleans. Natty left New Orleans late in 1861, returning to the Bruff Bros & Seaver offices in New York.

Natty's firm then opened a factory in Stonington to produce muskets and pistols for the Union Army. He returned to Stonington and became the secretary and treasurer of this manufacturing plant on the Atlantic Ocean end of Water Street from 1861 to 1864. In 1865, he left to join the Phelps Dodge firm in Chicago, which made boots and shoes. Three years later in 1868, he became a partner there.

Natty also began to have serious health issues at this time. He caught a severe cold in 1871 that weakened his left lung. He went back and forth between Chicago and Stonington trying to improve his health. Then it became clear that he was suffering from pulmonary tuberculosis. He went to specialists, but all they could do was help arrest the progress of the disease.

Uncle Nathaniel offered to take Natty on a trip to China, but his nephew had just become engaged to Harriet Wilder and went on a trip with her to Europe early in 1872 along with his father, Alex, sister Libby and brother Alex Jr. In October 1872, he married Harriet. Nathaniel wrote him on October 13, 1872: "Your alliance with Miss Wilder has my most hearty approval …with her sweet manner & lovable character [you cannot go] astray in taking one of the same lineage as a partner for life."[11]

Nathaniel Brown Palmer's will was not subject to probate, probably because his wife Eliza pre-deceased him and they had no children. He left his estate in seven equal parts to his three surviving siblings: Alexander, Nancy, and William, and his four nieces and nephews by Alexander and Priscilla: Natty, Alexander, Louis Lambert & Elizabeth (Libby).

Libby (1848-1929) inherited Pine Point when her father

Alexander died in 1894. Her three brothers had pre-deceased their father and left no heirs. In 1873 Libby married Richard Fanning Loper, Jr (1850-1914). They had four children at Pine Point, three of whom lived in the house for the rest of their lives. Libby's daughter, Elizabeth (1889-1981) brought her four children up there. The family had limited resources, and sold Pine Point in 1976, including most of its contents. That is how the golden figurehead from the *Great Republic* Captain Palmer brought back to Pine Point in 1854 ended up in the nearby Mystic Seaport Museum. When Historic Stonington acquired the Palmer House in 1994 it was in essentially the same condition as when built by Nathaniel and Alexander in the early 1850s.[12]

On October 31, 1876, Nathaniel took Natty and his wife, Harriet, from New York to San Francisco. While there, Natty suffered from the dry atmosphere in California, where the air was full of dust. He came down with a severe cold, suffered two hemorrhages, had trouble sleeping, and lost his appetite. They made a trip down the southern coast of California, but it did not revive him.

Uncle Nathaniel eventually persuaded the couple to leave San Francisco for China on the clipper ship *Mary Whittredge*, hoping the voyage in the sea air might be good for Natty. The clipper was captained by Benjamin Franklin Cutler, a friend from Stonington who lived on Water Street. The *Mary Whittredge* sailed for Hong Kong February 17, 1877.

Just prior to sailing, Nathaniel tried to get help for Natty from a Dr. Ferrand, who was visiting San Francisco from Detroit. The doctor reported to him: "There is but little chance for your nephew. He has had it for five years and this seems like a fresh outbreak…a trial must be made…the most desirable a voyage to sea."[13]

The captain of the *Mary Whittredge* gave his cabin to Natty and Harriet. Despite the care he received from his wife and the crew, Natty continued to be very ill, losing twenty pounds. Everyone was deeply concerned. His uncle Nathaniel commented: "He is a perfect skeleton, there is nothing left of him." They arrived in Hong Kong on April 19, 1877. From that point on, Uncle Nathaniel's health and spirits began to deteriorate as well, reflecting the condition of his beloved nephew. The group decided to sail back to San Francisco.[14]

A letter from Libby Loper, Alex and Priscilla's daughter, then twenty-nine years of age, describes what happened:

> The party sailed from Hong Kong for San Francisco May 15th in the steamship *City of Peking*, hoping Natty might reach home alive—but he died on the second day out. The body was embalmed and arrived home June 18th and was placed in a vault. After Natty's death, Uncle Nat began to fail rapidly. He seemed to be completely prostrated by anxiety and grief, together with slight hemorrhages. Before his ship arrived at San Francisco he had a severe hemorrhage losing two quarts of blood. The surgeon attended him constantly and said: "Any ordinary man would have died at once." On arrival at San Francisco he was taken to the Palace Hotel, lying there in a comatose state. He rallied at times and recognized those about him, seeming to suffer no pain.
> Uncle Nat died on June 21 1877 at age 77.[15]

On June 14, 1877, Natty's associates at Phelps Dodge & Palmer in Chicago had written:

> He was generous and frank by nature, and drew about him a host of friends. … He was very decided in his opinions, but with his firmness, gentle in his dealing with men, so that even those who most radically differed from him in business, religious or political views loved him. His love of the sea, and his boldness in facing danger of every kind were especially marked…He dearly loved his friends, his family, his home and Stonington.[16]

Captain Nathaniel Brown Palmer dedicated himself totally to

every cause, whether it was sailing to Antarctica, shipping men and guns for Bolivar, saving Eliza from the Chilean convicts, building the best boats for the packet trade between England and America, or inspiring and captaining ships for the clipper trade with China. He didn't do these things for fame or fortune, but because that was his job.

The sailors on board his ships immediately understood he was a man they could trust. He would take on any task asked of them, endure any hardship, face every risk, always striving to protect them. The women in his life, his wife, Eliza; sister Juliet; and sister-in-law Priscilla understood this too, as did his fellow investors in ships—E. K. Collins and his partners the Low brothers, clipper ship designer Donald McKay, and his nephew Natty.

Nathaniel's obituary in the *New York Sun* of Sunday, July 8, 1877, read:

> "The remains of the venerable sea captain … Nathaniel
> Brown Palmer and of his nephew N.B. Palmer
> were buried in the beautiful cemetery of this place.
> The funeral was from the mansion of State Senator
> Alexander S. Palmer, the Captain's brother … Many
> who loved the Captain and his nephew were there. The
> widow of the nephew leaned on the arm of her father-
> in-law, Senator Alexander Palmer … Capt. Nat Palmer,
> as he was lovingly known, had warm friends in nearly
> every seaport in the world … He began to command
> men even before he reached his majority … While he
> was a thorough disciplinarian on shipboard, he was
> gentle as a child in the family circle."[17]

THE END

ENDNOTES

CHAPTER 1

NATHANIEL PALMER'S BOYHOOD— STONINGTON, CONN.

1 Alex Roland, W. Jeffrey Bolster, and Alexander Keyssar, The Way of the Ship. Hoboken, NJ: John Wiley & Sons, 2008, p 87.

2 Thanks to Mary M. Thacher, former Stonington Historical Society (SHS) president and board member, who was responsible for its Woolworth Library. (M.M. Thacher, Claude Gabriel Family 1761–1815, HS Library).

3 Palmer-Loper Papers, LOC

4 John R. Spears, Captain Nathaniel Brown Palmer, New York, NY: The Macmillan Company, 1922, p. 6.

5 Steven Ujifusa, Barons of the Sea. New York, NY: Simon & Schuster, 2018, pp. 104–5.

6 Alexander Laing, Clipper Ship Men (New York, NY: Duell, Sloan and Pearce), 1944, pp. 91, 92.

7 Norman F. Boas, Stonington During the American Revolution (Norwich, CT: Franklin Impressions), 1990.

8 https://www.nps.gov/articles/privateers-in-the-american-revolution. htm#; National Park Service, August 4, 2023.

9 Theda Kenyon, That Skipper from Stonington (New York, NY: Julian Messner, Inc.), 1946, p. 14. 10 Alexander Laing, Clipper

10 Ship Men (New York, NY: Duell, Sloan and Pearce), 1944, pp. 66–67.

11 https://www.nps. gov/articles/impressment.htm#; National Park Service, September 21, 2023.

12 James Tertius De Kay, The Battle of Stonington (Annapolis U.S. Naval Institute), 1990; Hyannis, MA: Parnassus Imprints, September 1997, pp 6–8.

CHAPTER 2

WAR OF 1812—YOUNG BLOCKADE RUNNER *and* SEALER *in the* SOUTHERN SEAS

1 Laing, ibid, pp. 112–113.

2 De Kay, ibid, pp. 1–5; 9–12.

3 De Kay, ibid, pp. 13–20.

4 Roland, ibid, p. 128.

5 Benjamin F. Palmer, Diary of B.F Palmer, Privateersman (Hartford, CT: The Acorn Club, Tuttle, Morehouse & Taylor Press), 1914, preface on pp. xvi, xvii, xviii.

6 Nicholas Guyatt, The Hated Cage, Hachette (New York, NY: Basic Books), 2022. I am indebted to Guyatt's valuable book for much of our Dartmoor background material.

7 Norman Boas, M.D., Stonington During the American Revolution (Mystic, CT: Seaport Autographs), 1990, pp 48–52.

8 B.F Palmer, ibid, pp 199–200.

9 John R. Spears, Nathaniel Brown Palmer (New York, NY: Macmillan Company), 1922, p. 38.

10 Joan Boothe, The Storied Ice (Regent Press, Berkeley: CA, Regent Press), 2011, p. 23.

11 Boothe, ibid, p. 37.

12 William H. Kearns and Beverly Britton, The Silent Continent (New York, NY: Harper & Brothers), 1955, pp. 12–13.

13 New York Sun article on Nat Palmer's Life, July 8, 1877, Historical footnotes, Stonington Historical Society, February 1996, Vol XXXIII No. 1, p. 3.

CHAPTER 3
WHO DISCOVERED ANTARCTICA?

1 J.H. Parry, The Age of the Reconnaissance (New York, NY: Mentor Books), 1963, pp. 110–115; Samuel Eliot Morrison, European Voyages of Discovery (London, UK: Oxford University Press), pp. 136–148; Richard Dunn, Navigational Instruments (London, UK: Shire Pub Ltd, Oxford University Press), 2016, pp. 41–44.

2 John Blake, The Sea Chart. (Annapolis, MD: Naval Institute Press), 2004, pp. 20–21; Dunn supra p. 32.

3 Richard Henry Dana, Two Years Before the Mast (New York, NY: Penguin Classics), 1986, p. 62.

4 Photocopied from the SHS Library

5 Navigational analysis above; Michael Wiseman, Stonington Harbor Yacht Club Ex Commodore and blue water sailor.

6 HS Library

7 Edmund Fanning, Voyage Round the World (New York, NY:

Collins & Hannay), 1833, p. 435; Glenn Gordiner's Lectures at SHS on Nat Palmer "Discovering Antarctica." Online at https://www.youtube.com/ watchv=i6regXUMKo&t=1039.

8 Joan Boothe, The Storied Ice (Berkely, CA: Regent Press), 2011, pp. 37–8.

9 John R. Spears, ibid, p. 66.

10 Spears, ibid, pp. 72–75.

11 Palmer-Loper Papers, LOC

12 https://www.loc.gov/item/mm79034510

13 Volume XXX, Part 1, January 1939, Philadelphia, PA.

14 Volume XXX, no. 4, October 1940.

15 Boothe, ibid pp. 276, 277.

16 The Wall Street Journal, March 25–26, 2023, p. R 2.

17 Robert Silverberg, Adventures of Nat Palmer (New York, NY: McGraw-Hill), 1967, pp. 73–75; Lawrence Martin, ibid, pp 544–545.

CHAPTER 4

CARIBBEAN CHALLENGES—SAILING *for* SIMON BOLIVAR *and* EXPLORATION

1 Alexander Laing, Clipper Ship Men (New York, NY: Duell, Sloan & Pearce), 1944, p. 144.

2 John R. Spears, ibid, p. 104.

3 Robert Silverberg, Adventures of Nat Palmer (New York, NY: McGraw Hill), 1967, p. 80.

4 Spears, ibid, pp. 101–103.

5 Palmer-Loper Papers, LOC

6 Palmer-Loper Papers, LOC

7 Palmer-Loper Papers, LOC

8 Bradford-Fanning Papers, SHS Library

9 Palmer- Loper Papers, LOC

10 Bradford-Fanning Papers, SHS Library

11 Bradford-Fanning Papers, SHS Library

12 Palmer-Loper Papers, LOC

13 Palmer-Loper Papers, LOC

14 Bradford-Fanning Papers, SHS Library

15 Mary M. Thacher, The New Orleans-Stonington Connection in the 19th Century, SHS Library.

16 Spears, ibid, pp 115–129.

17 Silverberg, ibid, pp 84–90.
18 Spears, ibid, pp. 116–129.

CHAPTER 5

NATHANIEL *and* ALEX'S WIVES—CAPTAIN PALMER OUTWITS *the* CHILEAN CONVICTS

1 Palmer-Loper Papers, LOC
2 Palmer-Loper Papers, LOC
3 Jack Pearl, Captain Nat Palmer. Saga Books, March 1963, p. 68
4 Pearl, ibid, pp. 68–69.
5 Silverberg, ibid, pp. 95–98.
6 New York Sun article on Nathaniel Palmer July 8, 1877, Historical
    Footnotes Stonington Historical Society, February 1996, Vol
    XXXXIII No 1, p. 6.
7 John R. Spears,ibid, pp. 130–140, from Annawan Report of 2nd
    Mate G. Hubbard & the U.S. Counsel in Hong Kong F.T. Bush.
8 Palmer-Loper Papers, LOC
9 Palmer-Loper Papers, LOC
10 Palmer-Loper Papers, LOC
11 Palmer-Loper Papers, LOC
12 Palmer-Loper Papers, LOC
13 Palmer Loper Papers, LOC
14 Palmer Loper Papers, LOC
15 Palmer Loper Papers, LOC
16 David Cordingly, Women Sailors & Sailors Women (New York,
    NY: Random House), 2001.

CHAPTER 6

CAPTAIN NAT INSPIRES *the* BLUE WATER AMERICAN FLEET *to* COMPETE *with* ENGLAND

1 Silverberg, ibid, pp. 82–83.
2 Roland, Bolster,ibid, pp. 1, 27–33, 45–47, 7.
3 https://en Wikipedia/wiki Demographic History of the U. S.
4 Roland, ibid, p. 124
5 Silverberg, ibid, pp. 85–90.
6 John R. Spears,ibid pp. 163, 164.

CHAPTER 7
COMMODORE of AMERICA'S PACKET SHIPS *to* ENGLAND

1 Silverberg, ibid, pp. 103–105.
2 Carl Cutler, Queens of the Western Ocean (Annapolis, MD: U.S. Naval Institute), 1961, p. 208.
3 Laing, ibid, p. 65.
4 Silverberg, ibid, pp. 105–10.
5 Spears, ibid, p. 155.
6 Spears, ibid, pp. 143–163.
7 John R. Spears, ibid, p. 161.
8 Bradford-Fanning papers, SHS Library
9 Spears, ibid, pp. 166–167.
10 Robert Silverberg, ibid, pp. 101–113; Spears, ibid, pp. 141–167; and Jack Pearl, Captain Nat Palmer. Saga Books, March 1963, pp. 61–66.

CHAPTER 8
INSPIRER *and* MASTER *of* CLIPPER SHIPS *to* CHINA—THE HOUQUA

1 Spears, ibid, pp. 169–178.
2 Jayne Lyon, Clippers Ships & Their Captains American Heritage Publishing Co, New York, 1962,pp. 27–33.
3 Ujifusa, ibid, pp. 50–63.
4 Jacques M. Downs, The Golden Ghetto, The American Commercial Community at Canton, and the Shaping of American China Policy, 1784–1844 (New Jersey, London, & Ontario: Associated University Presses, Inc.), 1997, pp. 82, 151–159, 177–182. Useful facts and insight throughout.
5 Eric Jay Dolan, When America First Met China (New York, NY: W.W. Norton & Co.), 2012.
6 Downs, ibid.
7 Lyon, ibid, p. 33
8 Spears, ibid, p. 172.
9 Spears, ibid, pp. 170–176.
10 Mary M. Thacher's lecture to the Stonington Historical Society, January 13, 2005.
11 Silverberg, ibid, pp. 124–126; Spears, ibid, p. 176.
12 John R. Spears, ibid pp. 176-8; Low Family Papers, Peabody

Museum, Salem, Massachusetts.

13 Charles Clarkson Stelle, American and the China Opium Trade
in the Nineteenth Century (New York, NY: Ayer Co. Publishers),
1980.
14 Spears, ibid, p. 188.
15 Spears, ibid, p. 193.
16 Spears, ibid, pp. 185–189.
17 Spears, ibid, pp. 194–96.

CHAPTER 9
FAMILY TRAGEDIES—HOUSE FIRE, JULIET *and* PRISCILLA DIE
PREMATURELY

1 Palmer-Loper Papers, LOC
2 Mary M. Thacher, "The Stately homes of Lambert's Cove,"
Historical Footnotes, SHS, February 2001, Vol. XXXVIII, No. 1
p. 5.
3 Mary M. Thacher, verbal input.
4 Bradford-Fanning Papers, SHS Library
5 Palmer-Loper Papers, LOC
6 Bradford-Fanning Papers, SHS Library
7 Sarah Fanning's journal, New York to New Orleans November 1,
1844 to July 5, 1845 for several quotations (Bradford-Fanning
Papers, SHS Library)
8 Mary M. Thacher, note for SHS Library
9 Sarah Palmer Fanning Bradford journals (Bradford-Fanning Papers,
SHS Library)
10 From Sarah Palmer Fanning's Bradford's 1846 Hoqua journals
(Bradford-Fanning Papers, SHS Library)
11 Palmer-Loper Papers, LOC
12 Palmer-Loper Papers, LOC

CHAPTER 10
CAPTAIN PALMER'S SWAN SONG—CHAMPION *of* AMERICAN
WOODEN SAIL

1 Arthur H. Clark, The Clipper Ship Era (N.Y & London: G.P.
Putnam's Sons), 1910, pp. 82–86, 87.
2 Clark, ibid, pp. 96–99.

3 Material on Theodore and Harriet Palmer from research by Mary
   M. Thacher and Palmer- Loper Papers LOC.
4 Clark, ibid, p. 162.
5 Spears, ibid, pp 212–215.
6 Spears, ibid, 215–223.
7 Spears, ibid, 220.
8 Jack Pearl, Captain Nat Palmer, Saga Books, March 1963, p. 72.
9 Spears, ibid, pp. 239–240.
10 Spears, ibid, p. 246.
11 Spears, ibid, p. 248–249.
12 Clark, ibid, p. 232.
13 Clark, ibid, p. 292.

CHAPTER 11
THE GOLDEN YEARS

1 Palmer-Loper Papers, LOC
2 Palmer-Loper Papers, LOC
3 Palmer-Loper Papers, LOC
4 Palmer-Loper Papers, LOC
5 Palmer- Loper Papers, LOC
6 Palmer-Loper Papers, LOC
7 Historical Footnotes, HS Bulletin "Two Remarkable Seamen," New
   York Sun July 8, 1877,Vol. XXXIII No. 2, May 1996, p. 6.
8 Palmer-Loper Papers, LOC
9 Palmer-Loper Papers, LOC
10 Historical Footnotes, ibid, p 6.
11 Palmer-Loper Papers, LOC
12 Constance B. Colom, Administrator/Curator, HS Booklet- The
   Captain Nathaniel B. Palmer House.
13 Palmer-Loper Papers, LOC
14 Norman F. Boas, MD, Capt Nathaniel B. Palmer & Nathaniel B.
   Palmer 2nd—a Poignant Story, SHS Library, 1998, pp. 17-18.
15 Palmer-Loper Papers, LOC
16 Norman F. Boas, MD, Capt Nathaniel B. Palmer & Nathaniel B.
   Palmer 2nd—a Poignant Story, SHS Library, 1998, pp. 21-22.
17 HS Bulletin No 1, February 1996, p. 1.

INDEX

Harry F. Martin is a graduate of Harvard College and Harvard Law School. He began his career as a Wall St. lawyer, then served in the US International Aid Program in the Near East, Asia and South America. He ran the Merrill Lynch Bank in London and an Arab Consortium Bank in NYC, and then became CEO of the entity owning Cargill, Inc, America's largest family company. Before retirement he served as senior advisor to wealthy global families. He is the author of *Ernie O'Malley, A Life* (Merrion Press, Ireland, 2021), the biography of a 23-year-old Commandant-General of the Irish Revolutionary Army who fought Britain for Ireland's freedom from 1919-1921. For two decades Martin has given public lectures on a variety of topics, including: *Brush Up Your Shakespeare, Hemingway & His Four Wives, Generals Ulysses S. Grant and Robert E. Lee*, and *The Rockefeller Family*.

9 798218 469405